T0283554

The Book You Want Everyone You Love* to Read

Sane and Sage Advice to Help You Navigate All of Your Most Important Relationships

*(and maybe a few you don't)

Also by Philippa Perry

The Book You Wish Your Parents Had Read
(and Your Children Will Be Glad That You Did)

How to Stay Sane

Couch Fiction

The Book You Want Everyone You Love* to Read

Sane and Sage Advice to Help You Navigate All of Your Most Important Relationships

Philippa Perry

(and maybe a few you don't)

hachette
BOOKS

New York

First Published in the United Kingdom by Cornerstone Press, 2023

Hachette Go, an imprint of Hachette Books
Hachette Book Group
1290 Avenue of the Americas
New York, NY 10104
HachetteGo.com
Facebook.com/HachetteGo
Instagram.com/HachetteGo

First US Edition: October 2023

Published by Hachette Go, an imprint of Hachette Book Group, Inc. The Hachette Go name and logo are trademarks of the Hachette Book Group.

The Hachette Speakers Bureau provides a wide range of authors for speaking events. To find out more, visit hachettespeakersbureau.com or email HachetteSpeakers@hbgusa.com.

Hachette Go books may be purchased in bulk for business, educational, or promotional use. For information, please contact your local bookseller or email the Hachette Book Group Special Markets Department at Special.Markets@hbgusa.com.

The publisher is not responsible for websites (or their content) that are not owned by the publisher.

Library of Congress Cataloging-in-Publication Data
Name: Perry, Philippa, 1957– author.
Title: The book you want everyone you love to read: sane and sage advice to help you
    navigate all of your most important relationships / Philippa Perry.
Other titles: Book you want everyone you love to read (and maybe a few you don't)
Description: First US edition. | New York: Hachette Go, 2023.
Identifiers: LCCN 2023029482 | ISBN 9780306834868 (hardcover) ISBN
    9780306834875 (trade paperback) | ISBN 9780306834882 (ebook)
Subjects: LCSH: Interpersonal conflict. | Interpersonal relations.
Classification: LCC BF637.I48 P476 2023 | DDC 158.2—dc23/eng/20230722
LC record available at https://lccn.loc.gov/2023029482

ISBNs: 978-0-306-83486-8 (hardcover); 978-0-306-83488-2 (ebook)

Printed in the United States of America

LSC-C

Printing 1, 2023

This book is dedicated to all the people brave enough to write in to me at *The Observer.*

Contents

Contents

Introduction

I have worked as a psychotherapist for many years, and I have always thought it was a shame that psychotherapists tend to mostly talk about theories among themselves, behind closed doors. I feel so enthusiastic about how helpful these principles can be to people. From all the dilemmas and questions I get sent, I build up a picture of what people want to know about how to live their lives, and attempt to come up with some answers. So, my mission has been to bring these concepts and ideas into the wider world, and in my writing, I aim to share that wisdom in easily digestible chunks in the hope that more people can benefit from it.

This book is a culmination of many of the answers to questions that people have come to me with over the years, from my work as a therapist and an advice columnist, from talks and events, and from everyday interactions. I love your questions, because from your questions I learn where people have gaps. Although each person is unique, and the questions I get asked are usually very specific, I find that there are patterns and commonalities in those gaps and we can apply some generalized wisdom and techniques to them. Each question has taught me something and, maybe, I have occasionally helped you to have your own "aha moments" too.

As children, we all develop belief systems and adaptations that help us cope in our early environment. Often we might not even be aware that we are operating out of these systems, making decisions, and treating people according to these initial ways of seeing the world. As we grow older, meet new people, and experience more of the world, these belief systems and responses might no longer serve us in the way they did when we were young, and instead keep us stuck in old patterns of thought and behavior. What I hope this book will do is help you understand your own early adaptations and belief systems, and be more aware of where they are serving you and where they may need updating. Think of self-awareness as knowing where you are on a map: If you don't know your starting point you won't be able to figure out how to get to where you want to go. It's important that we learn how we react to the world, how we get angry, how we make assumptions about other people and how we talk about ourselves, because until we know what we are doing and how we are doing it, we won't know what we need to change.

When people first come to therapy, quite often they just want to talk about other people. What I tell them is that we can't do anything about other people, but we do have the power to control ourselves. Many of us don't understand we have that power: We can change how we react and how we respond. We can change our priorities, our belief systems, our habitual responses. Change takes time and new habits take a while to build up. But we can experiment with change, knowing that we have so much more power over our life than we realize. In particular, we have power over our own mind and where we want it to go. Even when we are at our most powerless, we still have the ability to choose how we think, how we organize our body, and how we relate to others.

Sometimes we might ask ourselves the wrong questions. We are forever asking, "Why?" because we are meaning-making creatures and we crave narrative. "Why did so-and-so break up with me?" "Why is my child misbehaving?" "Why do I feel so unhappy?" The emotional charge is all wrapped up in *why*—because we love stories and we love explanations. But asking yourself *why* is never usually very useful; the solution is normally in the *how*. What I'm interested in is *how* you are making yourself feel the way you're feeling: how you love, argue, change, and find contentment. That's why this book is structured in four "How" sections. These are separated out and we may think of them as individual issues, but they are all interconnected.

Being a psychotherapist has taught me that people grow in their own way and in their own time, in an environment where they can be themselves and where they are allowed to experiment with who they *can* be—as opposed to someone, or themselves, telling them who they *should* be. So my approach is along these lines. My definition of good advice is having someone put into words something that you have always known but haven't articulated yet. No one is always right. I'm not always right. And if you come across someone who thinks they are, there should be an alarm bell ringing for you, because the always-righters somehow have to make us into the always-wrongers—and that is not a nice place to be.

If I had to give you one piece of starting advice, it would be from that doyenne of self-help, Dr. Susan Jeffers, who said: "You are good enough exactly as you are, and who you are is a powerful and loving human being who is learning and growing every step of the way." In other words, you are acceptable just as you are, right now. When things work for us, we might not know how they are working for us, and it can be helpful to know that too. We can give ourselves such a hard time. This is not unusual. Every week I'm told "I'm no good at relationships," "I'm a terrible friend," "I'm not a clever person," "I'm too shy"...you get the picture. We don't need to judge ourselves like this. Yes, we have all made mistakes, but we are not our mistakes. We learn from them so we can go on to make new mistakes. We have a fantasy of what we want and need, and when we achieve our dream, the reality possibly teaches us it was a mistake. So we correct that mistake and learn from it, and then we go on to make another decision, it works for a while and then, after a time, we need to make another adjustment. It's not over until it's over and, until then, we can keep hoping, keep trying, and keep experimenting. When we find ourselves making a finite judgment about ourselves, when we put on that metaphorical black cap and bang the gavel and condemn ourselves, we don't do ourselves, or other people, any favors. Suspending judgment is nearly always a good idea. We all have a lot in common. We are all vulnerable human beings having to learn that there is more strength in knowing our fragility than clinging to a shiny shell of superficial ticks.

Finally, I hope you'll read this book in order to enjoy it. It may sound trivial but to enjoy yourself in life should be something we prioritize. If, as well as enjoying it, it resonates and you think *YES* and things fall into place, even just a little, then that's great. Obviously that's what I hope I'll achieve in this book. But your experience will tell you whether I've been successful or not.

The Book You Want Everyone You Love* to Read

Sane and Sage Advice to
Help You Navigate All of
Your Most Important
Relationships

(and maybe a few you don't)

1. How We Love

*Building Strong and Meaningful Connections
with Others and Self*

In Western society, we've come to believe that it's important to be independent. Stories of supposedly self-made entrepreneurs and stereotypes of the "modern independent woman" are everywhere. But I believe we are never truly independent: We rely on other people for just about every aspect of our life, from harvesting our food and getting it into the stores to supplying us with running water and building the houses we inhabit. It's a false construct to believe there is such a thing as complete independence. And just as we need other people to supply us with drinking water, we also need other people for company—even if some of us have tried to train ourselves out of this need.

As humans, unlike some other animals, we are not developed when we are born. We develop in relationship with our earliest caregivers—our sense of self, our identity, our needs, and our personality traits are shaped based on how we were cared for. The psychoanalyst and pediatrician Donald Winnicott said: "There's no such thing as a baby, there's only a baby and a mother." This makes us into creatures that need connection all our lives to feel like we are part of the wider world. Usually, that connection is with people, but we can also connect with ideas, places, and objects.

When I think back to my past psychotherapy clients, whatever their presenting problem was, I found that the origin of their concern was nearly always rooted in their relationships: how their past relationships had affected their belief systems, or their relationship with themselves, or how they were stuck in their relationships with others. I decided to begin this book with how we connect with others because it is the most important part of our lives. As people are dying, they will tell you that the most significant thing that remains in their life are their relationships, and these are usually relationships to other people.

Because we're complicated and all come from slightly different cultures—and by that I include general habits, family dynamics, languages, ways of doing things—relationships can be tricky. We all have different belief systems and ways of cooperating with one another. Finding a way through so that your relationships work for you and for the people around you might be essential, but it certainly isn't straightforward. That's what I hope this chapter will help you with.

Why We Crave Connection

Feeling connected to others is a part of being human. We need connection not only to other people but also to ideas, objects, and our environment. We want to feel that we're a part of something—whether that comes from meaningful conversations, small talk at the bus stop, reading a book, or watching something on television. This is partly why we are addicted to our phones: they give us a sense of connection that releases low levels of dopamine (the "feel-good" hormone).

However, if the only type of connection we have is via a screen, there is a chance we may begin to feel depressed, as we need more active ways of connecting where there is mutual impact between us and another person. If we are under-connected our mental health suffers. We want people in our lives who make us feel good, and we need people who support our current view of ourselves to confirm our identity. Connection matters because the people in our life are like mirrors in which we see ourselves. How others respond to us works as a sort of system of checks and balances for our mental health.

That said, there is also a danger in being over-connected. To explain this, there is a useful analogy that describes the human body being covered in hooks. If we have no hooks out, then no one else can connect with us and we can't connect with anyone, leading us to feel isolated and alone. But if *all* our hooks are out, then we're connected to everyone and everything all the time, and those individual connections stop having meaning or significance. We're jumping from person to person, idea to idea, and struggle to hold on to one in a meaningful way. Make a connection with everything and you'll discover that eventually you're not making a connection with anything. We've all met someone who is scattered and their attention is all over the place, who is difficult to follow or engage with properly, because you always feel like you don't have their full focus. This is what is known as manic behavior. It's fine to be manic sometimes—and for many it can be a route to creativity—but it's an unsustainable state to be in long term.

As with many things, there is a balance to be found. If we have a few hooks out—not all of them, but some—we can hook into who we care about and what we're interested in, and we can make sense of it. We can use our spare time to do what we find satisfying, be open to new people entering our life, and take the time to assess their values and whether they align with ours. It is a good idea to have people around us who make us feel positive about ourselves. People who, if they do challenge us, do so in a way that makes us feel enlightened rather than worse, and who are on our side.

> ### Everyday Wisdom
>
> Everyone needs to feel that they belong, maybe to a family, a project, a community, or to another person. We are creatures of connection, and we deny this at our peril.

In any group of people—any school, workplace, social group, or large family—subgroups naturally form. This isn't a bad thing or a good thing, it's just normal human behavior. Getting closer to a person or a couple of people means a subgroup forms and finding a place within a group can be formative for our sense of identity and belonging. The dynamics of groups means that not only do we mirror those around us to build a sense of who we *are*, but we also contrast with those outside our group to determine who we are *not*.

That is why being part of groups is so important, and why it can feel difficult if we find ourselves left out. A woman wrote to me because she struggled with this balance and found herself unable to initiate friendships with people beyond her husband and child, and the friends her husband had made.

> I am a thirty-two-year-old mom of a happy baby. I love him and I'm enjoying being on maternity leave. My husband is a lovely man who adores being a dad.
>
> We have nice friends, but they are friends my husband has made. I go to the baby groups and I chat to people, but how do you actually make friends with someone? I was hoping our prenatal group would be a good place to make new friends, but it is a bit cliquey—it felt like being back in school. It felt competitive and we don't have much money for all the baby accessories, activities, and classes. We went to a barbecue at one mom's house and it was a mansion and I'm embarrassed that our house is rented and small.
>
> People have commented in the past that they don't know me, or it's a shame they never got to know me. In

college, I focused on academic work rather than hanging out with people. I'm worried that if I don't get into a group of mom friends, it will start to affect my child because he won't make toddler friends or go on play dates and I want to give him every chance of happiness.

Firstly, this woman *can* do relationships because she seems to have two good ones—with her baby and her husband. What she is doing is something we can all be guilty of from time to time: making excuses because she is finding it hard to make a connection. She is being invited to other people's houses but is still seeing the groups and subgroups that form naturally as being "clic-quey," and thinking that they must all be competitive. In analyzing other people's behavior rather than her own, she has an excuse for why she cannot do anything to improve her connections. However, because we can't control other people's behavior but we can control our own, I find the best place to begin is by thinking about our role in the problem. How do we contribute to the situation if we haven't got a group to belong to? What is it that we do that makes us feel either too superior or too inferior to join?

Really, I don't think this woman wanted to make new friends. She was satisfied by the connections she already had, and her struggle is that she wanted to make friends for her son's sake rather than for her own. We don't all need the same number of connections—some people can get by with very few and this woman is an example of that. I don't know if it's possible to form genuine connections and alliances if you are not doing it for your own enjoyment and sense of kinship.

In order to connect with people, we need to use our courage to open ourselves up, share our vulnerabilities, and take care of others when they do the same. To really understand another person and to be understood, we don't have to be the same. We don't have to have the same feelings, or lack of feelings, the same label, or even hold the same opinions. But we do have to be willing to make ourselves vulnerable, to share how we experience ourselves and our world, our responses, feelings, and thoughts; we do need to be open to being impacted by the other person in turn. What is important is that we get close to understanding how someone feels, and feel for them, and be felt for in turn.

To truly connect with others we need to be not who we think we *ought* to be, or who we think they *want* us to be, but who we *really* are. If we never take the risk of disconcerting someone, we never give ourselves the opportunity of letting ourselves be known. To be known we have to be seen, and we will never be seen if we hide. Anxiety about how we come across can often get in the way of connecting. A way of circumnavigating that feeling is to supplant it by being interested in the person we've met instead. This means shifting our focus away from self-consciousness and toward curiosity in the other person. When we manage this, it becomes easier to be delighted in someone rather than drained by them.

One of the ways to increase wisdom and connection is to speak in the moment and work things out in conversation rather than thinking we need to have everything right before we speak. This means not filtering all your thoughts: Tell someone "I want to know you," or try to articulate other scary, self-revelatory thoughts without being certain how they are going to land. You can work out how you feel in relationship with another and not always in your own head. Say things spontaneously. Practice being yourself and being unsure how you'll be received. Dare to share. Is this a fail-safe formula? No. It is a risk. But it's a risk worth taking. If we only have a relationship with another person in our head, assuming we know how they will respond to us, we are not really having a relationship with them. When my correspondent talked of the others being cliquey or competitive, she wasn't relating to them: she was relating to how she imagined they were, and this is not how we connect.

If you do share who you really are and still find it difficult to find a group, then perhaps it is about looking elsewhere for your tribe. I think about how comfortable I feel in my life in London, where I am a part of many groups—some formal, like a choir I joined, and some informal, like groups of friends. Before moving here, I remember feeling bewildered, like I was often on the outside. I think that's because I hadn't found my people yet. The stereotype of moving away from a small town to a big city and finding your people there makes sense because with more people to choose from comes greater chances of meeting like-minded people whom you can connect with. And perhaps I hadn't found my people yet because I hadn't really found out who I was either. One of the best ways of finding out who you are is in spontaneous conversation with others.

Sometimes Relationships Feel Hard

Over the years, people have written to me about partners who think they're always right, friends who give them a hard time, parents who steer their life even after they've become adults, bosses who don't listen, and subtle bullies who have eroded their confidence with a thousand micro-aggressions until they're not even sure if the ground underneath them is the ground, or something they might drown in. Sometimes, we withdraw because relationships just seem too hard.

I think about a woman who wrote to me after lockdown ended because she was having a difficult time joining back in after a period of isolation.

> I'm only now able to get back into society after twenty months of having to isolate. Due to medical complications, I was only recently vaccinated and had been completely solitary out of fear of dealing with COVID-19. I was ill with a life-threatening infection at one point during lockdown and luckily got through that, but it showed me how alone and vulnerable I am.

I have also been made redundant. I have been applying for jobs, and going to interviews. Inevitably, I am being rejected, and even when I'm not, my value is being questioned and negotiated down.

I feel so let down by what I thought were solid friendships. Colleagues and friends dropped me when I could not offer them anything due to losing my job. You are totally on your own in life and relationships are all meaningless.

At thirty-nine, I've given up on the idea of a romantic relationship and having a family. Men want to know on the first date whether you're attracted to them—it takes me longer to know. It's as though there's no value given to nurturing relationships. I'm not looking for anything major, just responding either way to a text suggesting meeting up for a stroll, being available for a laugh and chat from time to time, or going on a date without expectations.

The door to the world might now be open but I am struggling to go through it.

Isolation and loneliness make us wary of others, distrustful. If something happens once or twice we can experience it as a pattern, and we withdraw to protect ourselves from it happening again. We become wary of being vulnerable to shield ourselves from further rejection. Human beings are pack animals, and when a pack animal is taken from their group and isolated then reintroduced, they don't throw themselves back into the center. They stay on the periphery, don't take risks, and remain relatively isolated. This experiment has been done with rats and with fruit flies. I don't think humans are much different as far as their instincts are concerned.

We can have some bad experiences dating or with people we thought were friends, and it's natural we think that this is a pattern and that all experiences will be like this in one way or another, proving that humans are somehow bad, and relationships meaningless. We can make very reasonable-sounding excuses—just like the aforementioned woman who presented me with her evidence. Reasoning can become our enemy when we use it to back up our instinct to shy away from new people after a period of isolation.

There are two things we can do with these feelings of fear and distrust: We can be ruled by the feeling and stay hidden, or we can feel the fear and join in anyway. If we hide, we carry on feeding our fears, but if we dare to feel them and act despite them, they will gradually diminish as we establish relationships and reenter the fray, even when we had believed we would not.

Sometimes we might be guilty of all-or-nothing thinking. We talk to ourselves with phrases like "no one cares about anyone else," "everyone is just out for themselves," "there is no point in any friendship." What these phrases have in common is that they leave no room for exceptions. They claim that life is either a 1 or a 10 and don't allow us to experience all the different permutations of 2 to 9, which are nearly always there. A good way to spot these all-or-nothing statements is if you are saying "all," "everyone," "100 percent," "no one," "never"—that's likely a fantasy, a theory, a familiar belief, and it needs challenging or changing. I've said it before and I'll say it again, don't mistake familiarity for truth.

Instead we could have a different fantasy. We could say "everyone is attractive and intelligent and interested in me." This isn't true either of course, but I always say, if you are going to have a fantasy, make it a good one. Which fantasy you have trained yourself to believe will impact what your energy is like with other people and what they will pick up on when they are with you.

Any supposition you do have about other people can become a self-fulfilling prophecy. When you go to a gathering of people and think as you enter the space, *Nobody likes me, no one wants to talk to me, relationships are meaningless*, how will that show in your body language? What vibes will you give off? You'll probably stay on the edges, avoid eye contact, and be guarded in any conversations. Now suppose you think

Everyday Wisdom

We can't help but imagine what other people's attitudes toward us are. But I always say, if you are going to have a fantasy about what someone else thinks about you, make it a good one. It might not change anything, but you'll be calmer.

instead, *Everyone is interesting and attractive and pleased to see me, and I'm interesting, valuable, and attractive. I want to talk to them about what I'm thinking, and I want to find out what they are thinking about*, then how will that show in your face, body language, eye contact, and the vibe you give off? It'll make you more approachable, friendlier, and relatable.

Our challenge is to not lose our faith in the inherent goodness of most people. Not all humans are all bad, and some of them are really great and will be fun and interesting. We can get into the habit of having relationships with others solely in our heads, and we imagine their motives, their thoughts, and their feelings to be the worst possible. We never actually check this out with them in reality, so we become our own persecutors but blame the other person for it. We've all done this. And we can stop doing it. Be optimistic about what people are like and gently push out the edges of your comfort zone, so that you can ease yourself back in and be less anxious. We have an advantage over the fruit fly—we can decide to acknowledge our instincts, understand them, and choose to override them. We can lead with our brain instead of with our instincts.

I get very excited about changing belief systems and the trick is to recognize when you are having a fantasy about a person or people. It is when you are cherry-picking the evidence to back yourself up rather than looking at all of it, and when you are using all-or-nothing statements. If you change a negative fantasy about others to a positive one it will show in your face and it will turn your life right around. I've done it, my clients have done it, and that's probably why I'm so evangelical about it. Reprogramming yourself from "everyone is horrible" to "everyone is lovely" can make the biggest difference in your life. You may find it easy or it may take all your courage to flip this switch. You'll need to turn your attention toward hopefulness and evidence that some seeds do germinate (but they won't if you don't sow them).

Now, repeat after me: "Everyone is interesting and attractive including you and me and we are all very pleased to see one another." It will take practice if you have acclimatized to "everyone is not worth the effort" because you've practiced that. Time to upgrade to your next self-fulfilling prophecy. We only have one life (apparently)—don't be a fruit fly.

How We Form Bonds

Often how we form connections in the present is influenced by how we were loved in the past. We seek partners who make us feel the same emotions we felt when we were around the people who brought us up. Sometimes people say love feels like "coming home," like coming back to what is familiar, from a time even before words could explain that familiarity. The trouble with what is familiar in this way is that it feels right. When we meet someone who evokes these feelings, it can feel like a spark, because we confuse what seems like good chemistry with what is familiar. That was the case for this man who wrote to me about his relationship problem.

> I was very much in love with my ex-boyfriend for the first three years of our relationship. Problems started when he asked me to marry him. I felt us disconnecting and asked to go and see a relationship counselor. It didn't help. He said some things in session that still smart today. For example, he said our partnership was like a whining child he wants to run away from. I became more distraught about the deterioration of the relationship as he became more distant.
>
> The wedding plans stalled. The final straw was him arranging a big vacation with his friend and I was not consulted or invited. I was desperate, and one day after he'd insulted me, I said I was ending it. Once I'd calmed down, I tried taking that back, but he wasn't having any of it. I never saw him again.
>
> Personally and professionally, I am now doing well. But I'm still haunted by feelings of grief, and I worry I'll not make it to a place where I no longer feel the pull. I need him to reach out and say he misses my friendship. I've had other relationships since that one, but I always have a sense that I'll never fully recover and will never fully be present in my life.

I'm guessing this man's ex had what we call in my profession an "avoidant attachment style." This means that he doesn't like to get too close—he might think he does, but he doesn't. It is not uncommon for people who have an avoidant attachment style to shy away from a relationship when it becomes more committed—even if they have initiated the commitment. People develop this style when they have learned in infancy that they cannot depend on others to soothe them. They solve that problem by unconsciously deciding (even before they can speak) that they will never need anyone. The defenses that helped us in our early environments become a hindrance and hold us back in new situations: What was self-preserving can become self-sabotaging. I might assume this man's ex finds the human need for connection frightening and/or repulsive to some extent.

The man writing the letter, on the other hand, may have what therapists call an "insecure attachment style." One of the main emotions insecurely attached people felt when growing up is longing—they longed for a parent's attention and now experience longing as love. It feels right because it feels familiar: Their earliest caregivers probably ignited more longing than security. Now this might sound far-fetched, but look at the way a toddler wants their parent. Notice the clinging, the desperation, the longing: It's all there. People with an insecure attachment style may be haunted by an inner ghost of that baby or toddler who longed and longed and sometimes had the ecstasy of being momentarily held in an intermittent way that reinforced the longing and made them long all the more.

People with this style are often attracted to avoidants and avoidant partners. Insecurely attached people are good at longing, and a lover who is likely to trigger it is someone who swerves commitment—in other words, someone with an avoidant attachment style. If we never seemed to get it right for our first caregivers, psychically this can feel like unfinished business, so we seek partners for whom we cannot get it right, with the wish that this time we will succeed, so the unfinished business can be laid to rest. Someone gorgeous who can never fully be there for us will ignite that fire. What is addictive about love for insecure attachment people are the highs, which are only possible because there are lows.

It's important to note that no one chooses their style of attachment—how we form bonds is an unconscious process. Nor is anyone stuck with their style forever—when you become aware of it you can choose not to be at the mercy of it. I believe the man who wrote to me, and people like him, can recover. If you relate to his situation, my suggestion is to go over your very first attachments with the people who brought you up—or who didn't but should have done—and see how relationships in your current life might push

Everyday Wisdom

We often mistake familiarity for truth. Just because we're used to thinking or feeling in a certain way, it doesn't mean it's right.

ancient buttons. Did you have to work hard to get the approval of a parent? Did a teacher you had a crush on withhold praise? Have you had a pattern of falling for unavailable lovers, those who lived abroad, or were already married?

If you find yourself in patterns of unrequited love, I want you to think about your longing. When you are in it, you are your longing. Your longing is you. Take a step back from it. Look at it in a detached way. To move on, what you'll need to do is recognize that your type is not your type. Your type of partner isn't the avoidant type who will give you these highs, followed by lows, but someone who is reliable, available, and dependable. This is what we call a "secure attachment" type. And it won't be love at first sight because they won't seem familiar in the way an avoidant person would be, but they're reliable. You won't get such highs, but you won't get the lows either, and over time, as you become more familiar to each other, you will slowly climb to a steadier high, built on the satisfaction of being in each other's company rather than the heady excitement of intermittent positive reinforcements.

Two Different Ways of Being Friends

Everyone will have their own inclination, habits, and beliefs when it comes to how we make and maintain connections, what we owe the people in our life, how we

should be with them, what is acceptable and unacceptable, loyal and disloyal—and we will differ from one
another. If we assume that others have the same ways of
being that we have, it's likely that it's our own assumptions and expectations that will cause us hurt rather than
others doing anything intentionally to reject us.

I receive many letters about two friends who were
once close and then one appears to let the friendship go.
This email from a woman detailing her friend's move to
America is an example.

> I have lost touch with the person I thought was my best
> friend. We met at school when she came for an exchange
> year from her home country. For ten years, she was the
> most important person in the world to me and we
> shared so much.
>
> About five years ago she went to America for a job
> and before she left, she visited me and it was wonder-
> ful. We had been struggling to keep in touch, as we
> started working and building our lives in our respective
> countries, but I never doubted her time on the other
> side of the world would only mean more for us to share
> with each other.
>
> She wrote me one postcard from America and I kept
> asking her parents for her address, so I could write to
> her there, as her email address no longer worked. But it
> never came. Through social media (via her brother, as
> she is not active online), I see she has now married her
> boyfriend who followed her out to the United States,

and that she lives back in her home country again and has had a baby.

It hurts massively that such big life events happened to her, and she seems not to have even thought about me. I wrote a letter to send to her saying how devastated I am (via the address of her parents' house, which I still know of by heart). I can't bring myself to send it, in case she never replies or tells me some horrible truth. Should I send it?

People's inclinations when it comes to friendships differ. Some are still best friends with people they played with in elementary school while others—although possibly pleased to bump into someone they once knew well—lean more toward forming closer bonds with people who are involved in their current lives. I'm not saying one way is superior to the other, or one is moral and the other not, just that these different ways of being in the world come naturally to each of us.

If you are naturally a good long-distant friend you may—like the woman who wrote to me—be baffled and hurt by a friend who has moved away and who lost touch with you. If you had done that, it would mean there had been some sort of hurt or a misunderstanding. And if you cannot think what that is you might assume they are being cruel or that you must be in some way unlikeable. It is just as likely that they have a different friendship pattern than you. If your friend is someone whose friendships tend to have more to do with the present than the past, they might be baffled to be told they have hurt you because they haven't been in touch. Their assumptions about friendship in general might not be the same as yours.

There are also those best-friend friendships that are almost like having a significant other, and then a real significant other comes along, a true love interest, and the best-friend friendship, it seems, was just a rehearsal for a full-blown sexual relationship. Again, this is fine if this was the case for both parties, but if one of you assumed your friendship was a bond for life and the other that such friendships are superseded by romantic love, there may well be hurt. Being someone's most important person might possibly be too much pressure. People's lives move and change, and priorities change with it.

Particularly as we get older, it can feel like going out becomes more of an effort; we might be more set in our ways and some flexibility of attitude may be lost. When we are younger, we are more likely to try out new things and bump into new people because we have more energy. Meeting at an older age might mean your habits and personality are more formed so you can expect bonding to be a more complex process. Lots of potential connections are out there and everyone is in a different psychological space, entering the fray with a different set of attitudes and wanting different things. I think it may be more difficult for older people to form a strong attachment, as young people can mature together. But it is far from impossible.

The Myth of Perfect

The writer Naomi Alderman said that the point of having a partner is to have a witness for your life. While there are plenty of people who can do life happily and successfully without a romantic partner, it is a different experience to do it together. Sophie Heawood, a single mother for years and author of *The Hungover Games*, told me that she recently realized that the point of a romantic partner is as much about your experience outside the home as the one you have with them in it. She explains that her experience out in the world has improved since knowing there is someone at home who loves her no matter what. "It's like wearing waterproof clothing after many years of feeling a bit too easily rained on," she says.

There's much research about the health and well-being benefits and costs of being in a long-term relationship and you could spend several hours googling it all. For me, one of the reasons for having a partner is to have a mutual, equal relationship with someone you love who accepts you exactly as you are and who loves you, faults and all. It's difficult under those circumstances not to grow as a person, not to have more courage, generosity, and love to give, not only to your partner but to everyone in your life. I imagine finding a loving partner as icing on a well-made cake: which is to say, if you prefer your cake without icing, that's fine too.

I probably get the most emails about how to find the perfect partner, particularly in today's world of online dating. This man is one of many who have written to me, struggling and exasperated.

> I've had some short relationships, been on many dates, and had one long-term relationship (a while ago now) where I was dumped on the day before we planned to get married. I put a lot of effort into online dating, but the final straw was sending quality personal messages to forty-seven different women over six months and receiving nil positive replies. I'm in my late fifties, slim, fit, tall, of average and conventional appearance, articulate, humorous, and intelligent.
>
> As well as online dating, I belong to a local social group for get-togethers and outings to meet people. I discount those who are too old, those who I wouldn't go on a seesaw with, and women who say "Done that and got the T-shirt" about relationships—and there's rarely anyone left.
>
> I've recently dated someone who talked long term, only to end it abruptly without giving a reason. This has been devastating. We only ever hugged, but this reminded me what is absent from my cold life.
>
> I have thoroughly disproved the saying "There's someone for everyone." There obviously isn't. Should I resign myself to being alone for the rest of my days? Or should I keep trying and hoping to meet someone special, knowing that repeatedly failing is damaging to my self-esteem and my mental health?

One of the mistakes I see people make is that they treat online dating like shopping: scrolling and swiping to find the perfect person, like they're searching for the perfect pair of jeans. I'm sorry to say that the perfect person is not out there. I advised the aforementioned gentleman to try to keep an open mind and embrace more of "I don't know" and less of being sure of what people are like and whether he'd get along with them. Put judgment to one side (people can smell "judgy" a mile away). Avoid putting people in boxes, and anyway, your type might not be your type.

It's hard to make a commitment in these times of internet dating because we have an infinite amount of choice. When we decide on something, we also end something ("cide" comes from the Latin *caedere*, which means to kill or strike down), and committing to a person means cutting off the possibility of other choices. It is natural to want it all, but to have a relationship that can grow into something means saying goodbye to the possibility of other people. Naturally, people do not want to make a wrong decision, but this fear of making a mistake may mean they stay on the fence.

Everyday Wisdom

Sometimes people try to avoid mistakes by not making a decision, but not making a decision is still a choice that has consequences.

The psychologist Barry Schwartz did experiments about how much the choice we have affects how we feel about the decisions we make. His research showed that when people have six chocolates to choose from, they decide quickly and are happy about their choice. When they have a hundred to choose from, most people do not go for the first one they are likely to enjoy, but agonize over all of them, and then when they eventually select one are much less satisfied with it than the people who only had a choice of six. Schwartz also found that people tend to be what he called either maximizers or satisficers (a portmanteau of "satisfied" and "suffice," essentially meaning "good enough"). The former hold out for perfection and the latter have a "that'll do" attitude. Guess who is happier overall? Yes, the satisficers. It is normal to worry that there is something better around the corner and therefore struggle to commit. And yet the choice we commit to will give us the most satisfaction because it is the commitment itself, as much as—if not more than—the object, that makes for a good choice. A maximizing tendency is your self-saboteur, not your friend.

If you are dating and struggling with feeling the pressure to find the perfect person, I encourage you to initially settle for someone in the ballpark instead. Think of love as something you do rather than something you fall into. And don't think of yourself as just the chooser, allow yourself to be found too. You'll need to get comfortable with that uncertainty. Put in less effort, go on dates and outings to have fun, and don't treat dating like an interview or a task. Be open, be you, and prioritize enjoying yourself.

The Fear of Forever

I received a letter from a twenty-four-year-old accountant studying for a master's while working part-time for a management consultancy. He told me:

> I recently met a woman on a dating app after being single for a year since the start of the pandemic. She's a similar age to myself and we've been dating for two months. She's very attractive and nice, and we have a good time together—she can make me laugh.
>
> There is a red flag, though. Although she is in her midtwenties she still lives at home and seems to have no plans or ambitions to move to living independently. Plus, despite having a part-time job, she doesn't contribute to the household bills. Now I understand that rent is high and people are staying with their parents for longer, but she isn't even planning on going to college or progressing further in her career. She spends most of her money on going out with friends, vacations, and hobbies.
>
> My friends and family say that she's a waster who will drain me of money if we ever move in together as she has never lived life like an adult, never had to budget or think about bills, and that I should ditch her. I can see their point, but I'm having a great time with her. It is hard to know what I should do. What would you advise?

I think many of us can relate to his situation: We've met someone we enjoy being around now but aren't sure whether they are the one we want to spend forever with. Society can often burden us with a board game of goals and milestones that we are supposed to reach by certain ages. Now this might be the best way of living for a lot of people, but it is not the only valid way to approach existence on this earth. We are allowed to enjoy ourselves in the present rather than predict the likelihood of being or not being with someone in the future. It is unfair and yet so easy to fall into fantasies of what may or may not happen, what we may or may not want, or what the other person may or may not do.

If you're in a situation where you have friends and family who are confused by your choices, I want you to know that it's good to listen and take it seriously when the people we are close to challenge us, and compatibility is important, but it is also OK to enjoy yourself in the moment. Take the time for things to run their course and to discover what that course will be.

It's important to remember a person is not just their prospects or their appearance. A person is a soul. Having the capacity to be happy, knowing how to have interests and friends, and connecting with someone else is worth a great many accreditations. We are what we like doing, more so than our qualifications. We cannot tell what a person is like or how they will impact our life just by what they look like on paper. However, we can tell whether we like someone or not by how we feel when we are with them. So I encourage you to feel and listen to what is real and working for you in the present rather than narrowing in on a hypothetical future.

If we don't listen to that and only stick to what we think we ought to be doing, we might be heading for trouble. I am reminded of Jane Austen's *Persuasion*. In it, the heroine, Anne, has been persuaded by the advice of an intelligent, sensible person whom she respects to turn down a young gentleman whose prospects are uncertain. (Austen herself had a young man interested in her who was persuaded by his father to choose someone who wasn't as poor. Maybe that influenced the novel.) *Persuasion* is a beautiful cautionary tale of the effect of following sensible advice that goes against the heart.

Obsession Isn't Love

A common mistake I see people make is to confuse obsession for connection. I partly blame Hollywood for celebrating the "falling in love" trope that we see in films: the kind of love where you are swept up in a passive way. It happens *to* you, really, like how it happens to a baby or a toddler. A small child doesn't do anything; they fall into longing.

This email from a woman who felt a missing "spark" in her relationship is a good example of that.

My partner and I are both thirty-three. We met around two years ago. He is a kind, attractive person, and from the start it felt safe, relaxed, and comfortable, but not especially sparky. This is still true. Yet the more we get to know each other, the more some things improve. Unlike some of my previous partners, he is sensitive, intelligent, consistently kind, caring, and generous— qualities I really value and, having had many negative experiences of dating in the past, can appreciate.

The problem is, there is some part of me that is unsure and I don't know why. I think I'd like someone who initiated more conversation or more adventure. I love and care for him very much. I enjoy his company and feel loved; we have good sex. It all seems to be there, but I want to feel more excited, more thrilled by the relationship. The sense of passion and excitement I had in previous relationships probably came from an unhealthy dynamic, because I never knew where I stood.

So, I don't know what to do and it is making me anxious. I feel like I am changing my mind every minute. I care for him and don't want to hurt him, so I don't want to talk about it with him. He says the relationship is great.

We are likely to be obsessed when we're not sure where we stand with someone and then, when they finally pay us some positive attention, we get a rush from it. On the other hand, when all we receive is positive attention it's easy to take that for granted. As I said earlier, there won't be the lows that are the reason for such highs. But what we have instead is a steady, slow build toward a longer-lasting high.

Often, people who are addicted to this kind of adrenalized love remind me of people who are determined to quit smoking or stop drinking. With an addict, there are usually two parts to them: the sensible, this-is-bad-for-me part, and the impulsive, unthinking part who reaches for the cigarette, the drink, the drug, or, in this case, the lover. They know it's bad for them, will damage their health, but without even putting it into words they find themselves lighting another cigarette; no decision-making process, they just do it. When we are addicted to drink, in our mind we think about what a first or a second drink used to feel like, which fuels the yearning. We don't think of how we feel the morning afterward, we don't dwell on not being able to stop once we start, we just remember the good bits, glossing over the gnawing unhappiness and the see-saw emotions. I often tell people who are addicted to adrenalized love that their type of romantic partner is not their type. Choosing a partner is not like choosing

> **Everyday Wisdom**
>
> People mistake love for something you fall into, whereas it is much more than that. Acting lovingly is something you do. Love is not just passive.

curtains. Curtains start off great and then they fade. A relationship continues to grow and build. Mature love is more about caring and doing things for each other than the heady, infatuated initial stage. It also means supporting each other to find fulfillment. A love like that? Wow! That is a different sort of love altogether. That isn't passive, that is love as a verb, that is love as an action, that is the sort of steady, committed, available, consistent kindness that is the love we need rather than the one we might think we want. Not the heady obsessional, no-one-has-had-a-love-like-ours craziness, not that raging sea, but a steady lake that runs deeper than we could have ever imagined. And the old, old scar that formed from childhood will heal and—more than heal—will become memory upon memory of love in action rather than love that falls down a familiar hole again. Don't fall into the longing trap, *be* loving. It's far better in the long run and leads to something more sustainable.

Aristophanes, in his account of the origins of love, imagined that humans are cut in half by the gods and everyone has the perfect other half out there—all we have to do is find them. He has a lot to answer for because we are never cut in half—and there is no perfect match. But three things can help. First is commitment: A relationship is far less likely to work without it, because instead of working through problems, you are more likely to run away. Second is taking responsibility for your own feelings rather than thinking your partner is responsible for them. The third thing is time. The letter writer said, "The more we get to know each other, the more some things improve." This is what long-term love is about, not the thrilling uncertainty of "he loves me, he loves me not."

A Relationship Is More Than Sex

I recently received a letter from a woman in her seventies who has been in a relationship for nearly two years. Everything has been going well and she sees long-term potential in her new partner, except for one thing.

> I am a deeply sexually alive person. Sex is an immense joy to me. Not only the explicit physical acts of it, but also the sharing, the play, all the openness and open-heartedness. My partner is divorced and I suspect has not had much sexual experience. I think he is sexually repressed. I have always been open with him about wanting our relationship to become fully sexual. It never has been.
>
> He has a serious heart condition and wants everything we have, minus a full sexual relationship, for fear of his heart, although his doctor has given him the green light and said he's fine to use Viagra. It troubles me that my partner responds to my talking about wanting a full sexual relationship in offhand ways, uncaring about my needs and wishes—in every other way he's the person I have been waiting for.
>
> It seems like a no-brainer: I should leave. But we are compatible in every way other than this, including intel-

lectually. We are both in our early seventies—when it's far from easy to find a compatible partner. The grief of not having sex again would be immense, plus maybe underlying resentment would likely erode my regard for him.

I fantasize about finding a part-time lover, to live that part of who I am, while being with my partner for the rest of my life in every other way. Would he go for it? Maybe, but I doubt it.

Partner relationships could be seen in phases. They might look like the following:

- Pre-sexual, not cohabiting
- Sexual, not cohabiting
- Sexual, cohabiting
- Post-sexual, cohabiting

Of course, some people are never post-sexual, but when we're in our older years, we won't be sexual as often as when we were younger, and infrequent sex happens sometimes gradually and sometimes in bigger steps, like when we have a child or get sick. It can rock our sense of security when sex

> **Everyday Wisdom**
>
> Just because a drop in sexual frequency might happen if a couple grows apart, it doesn't follow that they are growing apart if they have less sex. What is important is honoring bids for attention, sexual or not.

becomes infrequent because, quite often, it's a strong mutual physical attraction that got us into the relationship in the first place. Don't confuse infrequent sex that happens naturally over time with infrequent sex that happens when you've got a difference you cannot reconcile.

A sexual relationship can so often be about status in one way or another. What I mean is that a relationship can fall into a destructive cycle and become more about who has the power than it is about mutuality, support, and enjoyment. If we're not careful, what was a close relationship can descend into "who's best" in some way. These things are not often talked about or acknowledged unless you are psychologically minded, and in a couple it can be very complex.

There's often work to do in terms of the boundaries each person needs and where compromises need to happen. I do believe that someone who doesn't want to have sex shouldn't be pressured into it. We cannot reason with someone about not wanting to have sex. Yes, this might be heartbreaking and frustrating for their partner, but we are each responsible for caring for our own bodies and discovering what we each need.

Some of us tend to assume that sex means the same thing to our partners as it does to us. This is not done consciously but in a sort of take-it-for-granted way, and it is often left unsaid. It's why it can be a shock when differences are found in how someone else approaches intimacy, sex, and masturbation. The thing to remember is that each of us will have formed different attitudes to sex; this might be difficult to explain or talk about because many of us might not have been in the habit of putting nonconscious assumptions about sex into words (perhaps not even to ourselves). But I do think it's important to really understand what is on our respective pages and to have sympathy for each other's points of view. Beware of seeing issues in terms of right and wrong, and keep the dialogue open.

I'm afraid our bodies do reach a peak condition in youth and, as we age, we are allowed to mourn the loss of taut flesh, just as we are allowed to mourn the fact that sex is no longer a twice-daily occurrence. But this will not dent our capacity to love and appreciate our partner as much as we ever did. And, occasionally, such a body, with its bulges and aches, will also be the vehicle with which we enjoy great sex—maybe not as often. What sustains a marriage isn't regular, terrific sex; it is honoring bids for attention. What I mean by this is that when one of you makes a remark (it need not be about sex; it could be as mundane as a comment about the cat), or seems to be asking for a response, that reaching out— the bid—is responded to, or, in other words, honored. Honoring doesn't necessarily mean doing what the other person wants, but it does mean listening and communicating that you've understood them. Research from the Gottman Institute has shown that when seven out of ten bids in a marriage are honored on both sides, the marriage will do well; less than three bids for attention honored and a marriage is likely to be in trouble.

Another indicator of a good marriage is loving touch—which isn't necessarily sexual touch. Feeling relaxed with each other means we can share thoughts and feelings. Not feeling competitive with each other too often and not getting into a frequent scramble for the moral high ground also helps to make for a long-lasting, mutually supportive bond. Over time, a couple shares so many things together, such as memories and bringing up children, that their love is less likely to be demonstrated through sex. Other things can gradually take the place of sex as bonding agents. It is those other things that happen in a relationship that keep it together, like enjoying each other's company. Companionship, in the end, is what most people probably need even more than sex. A compatible companion needs treasuring.

That said, our protagonist decided that sex was too important to her to give up. In a follow-up note, she told me that she left her partner because he did not want to share her with a lover. She is now seeking new pastures. Time will tell whether it was the best decision for her. I'm not always right.

The Power of Surrender

I once had a client who would tell me about incident after incident when he was right and the other person was wrong. At first I was sympathetic, but when I had listened to many similar stories, I realized something was stuck.

He had been reluctant to tell me about his past, his childhood, and he was convinced that his problems were in the present, specifically "other people." I told him I felt frightened that soon I would be made into one of these other people, and indeed that did happen. On one occasion, I got the time wrong for our session—which was erroneous, careless, and regrettable on my part, but my client wanted to make me into a monster because of it. Four sessions of him telling me how bad I was got very wearing for me. Eventually he ran out of steam and started to go back to stories of other wrong people in his life, and I encouraged him to tell me about the first person who got it wrong for him.

At that point, he opened up about his mother who had not believed him when he'd told her that he was being sexually abused. His mother failed to protect him and put him in danger time and time again until eventually he was old enough to leave the situation. This was the injustice of his life, and it was painful for my client to face it. He felt as scared, angry, vulnerable, helpless, and hurt as he had while the abuse was taking place. No wonder he had been so reluctant to remember, but when he did—when he went over the abuse he had suffered and realized he was now an adult and in control of his life—the need to blame other people for everything began to fade. He began to have better relationships, less conflict, and a better work life. I was even allowed to get things wrong occasionally without being made into the devil.

My client did what we are all capable of doing: living in the present with a past dynamic. When he learned to leave that dynamic behind, he became capable of allowing the influence and impact of others. He was able to let go of the pride of always being right and learned how to trust and surrender. He had discernment, of course—he wouldn't surrender to just anyone, but to just enough people to allow love into his life.

To those who know and love us we are special, but this doesn't make us more special than any other human soul. When he first came to see me, my client had an unshakeable belief in how very special he was that led to him always being right. This undesirable trait has been recognized in humans for centuries. In olden times it was called the Sin of Pride and indeed Oxford University has held an annual sermon on this sin ever since a past student left a legacy to fund it in 1684, so I'm telling you nothing new.

When I was asked to deliver this sermon in 2022, I accepted, not because I had wisdom burning me from the inside that I had to impart, not because I wanted to help out, but for retribution. For most of my life I have been an undiagnosed dyslexic, and my dyslexia stems from something called auditory processing disorder. This means I can hear all sounds distinctly but there is a slight delay before I can make sense of them. Prior to all these fancy diagnoses coming into vogue, I was merely categorized as "not very bright." I was slow to read, was a Mrs. Malaprop, and could not spell. I was certainly not of the caliber of pupil to go to college and definitely not

Oxford. My parents thought it would be a good idea to get me married off to someone who did, so I was sent to the Oxford and County Secretarial College in St. Giles. Sending a dyslexic on a shorthand and typing course before the invention of spell-check would, in my estimation, fall into the category of "not very bright," and I failed.

Despite the shortcomings of my education, I have held down jobs, become a psychotherapist, written academic papers and books, presented documentaries, podcasts, and radio shows, and have a weekly column in a national newspaper. I make a living from the words that used to be my torture. But despite this apparent success my pride is still wounded from that early "not very bright" label. So when I was invited to give this sermon, I wanted to show my now dead elementary-school teachers that maybe I was just a tiny bit bright if I was given the honor of delivering a sermon *at Oxford*. The irony that the sermon was about the sin of pride is not lost on me.

I interpreted the sin of pride to have many parallels to what we tend to refer to these days as narcissism. No one is born narcissistic or prideful; we are trained in these arts by our upbringing. Most often it happens as a consequence of seeing ourselves or our family being treated as superior during childhood, or alternatively being treated as if we were nothing, pushing us to compensate. Narcissists see themselves as either "the best" or "the most" and want to be treated as special. An overinvestment in self-image is a symptom of narcissism. And narcissism has become the norm in our society. The proliferation of material things has become a measure of progress; wealth occupies a higher position than wisdom; and notoriety is more admired than dignity. Our politicians, our institutions, and our culture are steeped in narcissism—we have a culture that overvalues image at the expense of truth.

That said, not all pride is narcissistic: We can be proud of our children, our friends, and our achievements. But we shouldn't get into the habit of believing our people or our achievements are superior to someone else's. That is when our pride stops being healthy and starts being at the cost of someone else.

Surrendering is an antidote to prideful or narcissistic tendencies. R. D. Laing coined the term "diaphobia," which he defined as a fear of true dialogue: in other words, the fear of being impacted upon or influenced by another person. To surrender is to let go of that fear. For example, surrendering control of a conversation would mean not trying to manipulate the other person but being open to the impact of them upon you. To surrender is also to offer something of yourself to the other without knowing how it will land with them. It means lowering your guard, allowing yourself to be vulnerable. It means surrendering to the inevitability that other people will not see you as you might want to be seen. It means not demanding of them that they see you as this or that, and not focusing on what you're going to say next while someone is talking. Instead, surrendering is opening yourself up to how their words may affect and change you. When you surrender to a conversation you don't know where it will lead because you are open to any outcome. It also means allowing and trusting others to be as they are.

To surrender to another person is a risk and an act of love. Surrendering means losing your ego, letting go of controlling behavior, and having faith that what will be, will be. When we surrender to a group process, we may feel uplifted as we will experience being part of something bigger than ourselves. To surrender to others is to give ourselves the opportunity to become something greater than our individual self. This isn't about being conquered by a more powerful person—instead, it is about letting go of a rigidity that stops you growing in relationship with others. Of course, there is risk in this act of surrendering. Surrender to a shark and you will be a shark's dinner. But if we don't risk surrender, we risk remaining unconnected, unable to fully contribute to the wider world.

When we define another person as being narcissistic, or of being this or of being that, we are placing ourselves in a superior position to them. So, what are we supposed to do? Instead of defining the other person, we define ourselves. Instead of saying "he is a bully," we could be more personal and specific in our feedback and say "I feel intimidated by him." Another way to think about this is to put judgment to the side. So instead of saying "Oh, that was excellent"—which again places us in a superior judging position—we can instead give words to our experience, such as "I was enlightened by that experience," or even "I enjoyed that," or "I was uncomfortable during that." Rather than judge something as good or as bad—making our subjective experience sound like objective judgments—I believe we only need to describe our personal reaction. There's a difference. Perhaps we might not manage to do this all the time, but that doesn't mean we can't aim for it.

I'm also wary of the type of pride that grows from its opposite: shame. This is when we feel proud because of a past injury, such as my being proud of writing books and having a column because I once failed to pass a typing test. It has a tinge of revenge to it, of anger even. It is as though I want my now dead teachers to feel the shame I was made to feel. There is no humility in that. We automatically react to minimize our potential shame as though shame would annihilate us. But if, instead of just reacting, we thoughtfully and truthfully reflect on situations and our role in them, we would find that shame does not kill us. Swinging into pride from shame is the same as

> **Everyday Wisdom**
>
> Even if you have long lost contact with the person who has harmed you, when our psyche gets used to having an enemy, it will seek another. This is an obstacle that needs to be overcome if we are to build strong connections with others.

swinging into narcissism from childhood mistreatment. Letting go of pride and welcoming in humility looks a little like replacing control and judgment with a little more surrender.

Maintaining a Strong Sense of Self

While connection to others is a fundamental human desire, it's also important to have our own interests so we can get our sense of self from things we enjoy and not just who we are to others. This is particularly heightened with parents. Being a parent—or a sibling, or a lover, or a friend— isn't being just one type of person. None of us is set in stone—humans are more flexible and changing than that.

Any healthy relationship between two adults means supporting each other to find fulfillment outside the relationship. If the caring and support is only going in one direction, it doesn't look like a mutually loving relationship—it looks like one person in the relationship is being a martyr. I'm here to tell you, don't play the martyr. You can be ambitious and strive for what would fulfill you—and you can even do that *and* stay in a happy partnership.

I received an email from a woman who married her husband young and quickly after a whirlwind summer. She had just turned seventeen and he was twenty-one. It felt like the greatest love affair of her life and he opened up a world of freedom in which she could discover herself—parties, being on the road, and so many wonderful, interesting people.

> Fast forward twenty-plus years and two children later and I sit here looking at my life, yearning for that summer of love again. To go back to that happier time. Instead, I find myself full of regret, with resentment bubbling deep inside.
>
> We live in isolation, with no friends. Socializing is expensive and with only my income for the past fifteen years, it is one of the sacrifices we made. Work used to be my escape, my chance to be with other people, but since the pandemic hit, I've been working from home and this is now permanent.
>
> During this time, I have discovered I can't stand my husband. I still love and care for him deeply, but I can't bear to be around him. I'm ambitious and want to be free to do things. He wants me tied to the house serving him.
>
> We have very different ideas of what our partnership should be and no amount of talking, explaining how I feel, acknowledging his feelings, ever seems to change anything.
>
> I fear we are no longer compatible. I don't want to lose him, but how long do I go on being unhappy in myself? I've dedicated my entire adult life to him—his needs, making him happy. When do I get to be happy?

It often happens in a relationship, especially if at the start one person steps into the I-am-older-and-wiser role, that the other person contorts themselves into any shape to try to please their partner, losing themselves and their own wants and needs in pursuit of this. I can understand— bonds are precious. A sense of kinship is invaluable. But losing ourselves to fit in with who others think they want us to be can lead to loneliness and depression. We need to be our authentic selves with other people for most of the time, not the person we feel we ought to be, or we run the risk of feeling unsupported, isolated, and discon- nected. When we learn to reflect more, we can let go of guilt. When we become more self-aware, we learn how to recognize our own needs.

As a general suggestion, I encourage everyone to reflect on their life beyond any single relationship—to think about friendships, work, other interests—and whether they have ever been allowed to know what they want. We often talk about finding the right romantic partner or finding "the one"—and our society is organized around this idea of a partnership—but I often wonder if happiness is more easily found in groups. It's hard for one person to fulfill all our needs in the way that multiple connections can, and placing all our energy into a single relationship can lead to becoming overly dependent on that person.

Adapting to other people is a skill. Some people need to learn how to adapt and turn up the adaptation dial while others need to turn it down. If you adapt so com- pletely to the other person, putting in more effort to work out their feelings than giving yourself attention to work out your own, there is nothing left of you for them to have a relationship with. It is even hard for you to have a relationship with yourself. Setting boundaries with others is key in having a strong relationship with yourself. If people have a good sense of where your boundaries are and do their best not to cross them, there is little need to define yourself by explicitly saying what you will and won't tolerate. We don't normally set terms and conditions in relationships—romantic or otherwise. Usually, we instinctively understand how not to tread on one another's toes, but sometimes boundaries need to be spelled out.

You must decide where you are going to draw the line and be clear about it. Whenever you put a boundary down with anyone, you need to know where your own limit is. When you have a boundary in place, you don't have to be cruel about it, you can put it in place kindly and explain why you need it, but you must be sufficiently resolved to keep that boundary. Putting down this line in the sand may be difficult, especially if you don't have much practice, because we all have plenty of conditioning to overcome. Growing up, many of us never got permission to be anything other than obliging. This is fine if everyone respects one another, but if respect is lacking it gives those who disrespect an unfair advantage. The person you really need to be kind to is yourself, not someone who seems intent on ignoring your wishes. One reader of my column once left a comment saying that if you have to choose between guilt or resentment, choose guilt. Wise words. And this is what I urge you to do—choose guilt.

When we fall for someone, we trust them and to some extent surrender our power to them. This is normal: This is falling in love. It should be equal, mutual, and generally lovely. However, when the surrender is one-sided, it puts us at risk of coercive control. Women's aid charities describe coercive control as an act or a pattern of acts of assault, threats, humiliation, and intimidation or other abuse that is used to harm, punish, or frighten their victim. We need to be able to spot these signs of abuse, but abuse exists as a relational dynamic rather than a list of possible behaviors. It is a pattern of harms committed with the intent of controlling the behavior of another person and can take many different guises, such as not wearing something because you're scared your partner will kick off again. It's also important to note that controlling relationships such as this are not confined to couples but exist within families and friendships too.

When we are controlled by another person, it erodes our emotional well-being and we become trapped. The person we see the most becomes like a human mirror for us, and the image they reflect back to us is distorted, eroding our confidence and well-being even further. It is hard, and the longer it goes on, the harder it gets to leave. Coercive control is dangerous, and if this rings bells, get help. My suggestion is to make a plan, and carry out one step of that plan at a time. Don't tell the other person what you're doing until you're safe.

Remember, you were not born merely to serve and get it right for other people; you can be your own person and get it right for you too. When you set boundaries, get more of your needs met, and reach for your goals, when you get to know and respect and love yourself, people might just change in response to that and learn to love and respect you too. If you give yourself permission to live the life

> **Everyday Wisdom**
>
> If you have to choose between guilt and resentment, choose guilt. You will discover that your world does not fall apart.

you want without anyone's blessing, and get to live it, it is very likely you will find greater satisfaction and closeness within your relationships as well. You may discover that your relationships become stronger and more authentic as a consequence.

Going back to the woman who wrote to me—she can give herself the freedom to live the life she wants, even without her husband's blessing. In fact, in doing so she's very likely to find him less irritating than she does now, and she might even warm to him again. He might discover too that his world does not fall apart when she gets more of her needs met. Connection is important and we need to be connected to more than just one person. I believe we need other people and we need the wider world.

If someone in our life is coercing us to never change things or otherwise forcing us to live a life we don't wish to lead, then we need to get out. But if we are just waiting for people to agree with us, then we must do whatever it is we want to do. Those people have a choice about whether to stay with us or leave. I'm not going to suggest ways of bringing them around, that is not the point—the point is that we must do what we need to do so that we get to live our best life rather than simmer with resentment. The time to be happy is now.

I want to be clear that there is no right way of "doing" relationships—there are as many ways of building strong and meaningful connections as there are combinations of people in the world. But I hope that the examples in this chapter have given you new insight into how you form relationships, how they are already working for you, and perhaps how you might decide to make some changes.

When someone has a personal problem, even if initially it doesn't seem to be about how they relate to others, go a little bit below the surface and you'll find that their personal problems are usually relational problems. This is true for anxiety, depression, and paranoia because we form in relationship with others. Get our relationships on a more functional and even keel, and we'll become more functional.

It can be easy to believe that other people are the problem when we're negotiating our relationships, yet most of the time it is a combination of others and ourselves, which means our connections aren't as strong as we might hope. Conflict in relationships is never easy to negotiate, but it does come with the territory, and it's this that I want us to think about next.

2.   How We Argue

Coping with Conflict in Our Personal and
Professional Lives

No matter how much we work to have better relationships with others and ourselves, no relationship is without
its challenges and arguments. Learning to navigate those
tricky moments doesn't mean that you will stop disagreeing with the people around you. The reality is that there
will be conflicts in any relationship as we all experience
things differently. No matter how similar two people are,
we each have our unique history and approach to things.
Everyone will have an individual experience of the same
situation, and just because they are different, it doesn't
necessarily mean anyone's viewpoint is more or less valid
than another's.

However, there are ways we can manage those situations of conflict and misunderstandings with our partners,
friends, family, colleagues, so that they don't feel tortur-
ous. By understanding how we argue or overadapt, and
by being more aware of where the emotional charge in
situations of conflict comes from, we can each work to
become more compassionate and open, and ultimately
reach stronger resolutions.

Different people argue in different ways and about different things, but there are some general patterns that I

have observed. As you read through this chapter, I hope you'll keep your eyes open to which argument types feel the most familiar to you. Do you find yourself getting stuck in dead ends because you think one person is right and therefore the other is wrong? Are you conflict avoidant and tend to let everything go, even the things that really matter to you? Do you fall back on arguing about facts and logic at the expense of listening to feelings? Of course, there is crossover between different types of arguments— and normally a single argument will be a combination of these modes—but I hope that by exploring them in this way, you might gain greater self-awareness.

Argument #1: Thinking, Feeling, Doing

It may be easier to understand another's experience if you can see that we each have a dominant—or preferred— way of coping. These are usually thinking, feeling, or doing. Some of us like to think our way out of trouble. Others need to explore their feelings first. And others go straight into action mode. I imagine these three ways of being as doors, and what we need to know is which are open, which are closed, and which are locked.

If two people have different dominant ways of coping, they might find it difficult to tackle problems together without arguing or disagreeing. I received the following letter from a woman who wrote to me after her husband had a stroke.

My husband is a sixty-something scientist and used to solving everything with his mind, but he has had to work hard physically to recover his walking. He's gone from a wheelchair in hospital to a walker at home and is now using a cane. But he's getting frustrated at his slow progress as he wants to think his way out of this and not exercise his way back to health.

I feel like I've been nagging him to do his exercises and feel more like his mother than his wife these days. I find myself getting angry and resentful at times, because he's not sharing anything emotionally with me (he never was good at it before, so I don't know why I would expect it now) and I feel very remote from him.

I've tried to talk to him about expressing his feelings, but he's just not interested. Then I feel guilty for having bad feelings about him, because he's the one who's suffering. It's been an exhausting time for us both. It looks like he will fully recover, but it's taking time.

Reading her letter, I think that her husband sounds like he has his thinking door open, his doing one closed, and his feelings one locked. She, on the other hand, sounds like she has her feeling and doing doors open, but her thinking door is more closed. The conflict between her and her husband—the resentment and anger that she describes—is a result of them having different doors open. In other words, they have different ways of coping.

When we find ourselves in difficult situations, we want the ones we love to be more like us. To react more like

53

us. But this woman's husband has got enough on his plate and can only cope with being himself at the moment, let alone take a leap and approach his life and recovery in the way she would. Remember, we are different and often it is these differences that draw us to others. We have a tendency to want or admire qualities in others that are underdeveloped in ourselves, but when a crisis comes along, we get het up because they are not more like us. It is normal to become less flexible and more set in our preferred ways when life's troubles arrive—like an illness in the family or challenges at work. It is as though we go into an emergency mode and become more rigid, more entrenched in our normal mindsets, and we become less able to see the situation from another's point of view. Back to our example: Once the woman understood her husband's dominant way of coping, she was able to find a "thinking" approach to nudge open his "doing" door: she got a medical professional to explain how new neurological pathways are formed through his prescribed exercises, so he could "think" his way into doing them.

When someone is ill, or in trouble, we may be tempted to give them advice and tell them what we feel they should be doing. We may believe that if the other person would only do what we say, or see what we see, then they would be better off. Often our motivation comes from not wanting to feel so much for them—their helplessness, vulnerability, pain, and frustration can remind us of our own. We don't like feeling these difficult things with them and so we give advice instead. However, for many people, being on the receiving end of unsolicited advice can feel like being judged or pushed away. Instead, we usually want to be felt with and understood. Think about it: If your dog is run over, you'd rather someone felt for you in your grief than advised you on how to hold a dog lead. Empathy doesn't mean trying to push the other person's feelings away or to fix them: It means feeling what they are feeling. This is not always easy, especially if their way of feeling things is different from yours. In our example, the patient struggled to share his feelings but could share his thoughts, and once his wife understood and empathized with that struggle, she was able to resolve their conflict.

I have found it is often a child's whining or crying that triggers impatience or even rage in a parent. It is easier to fall back on anger than to allow the child's feelings to awaken memories of our own childhood vulnerability, or to acknowledge the shame of feeling impotent in a situation we are incapable of making better. It may be more comfortable for us to persecute or patronize rather

> **Everyday Wisdom**
>
> There are three main styles of coping: thinking, feeling, and doing. If someone you love is going through a difficult time, try to understand what their coping style is and then feel with them rather than trying to deal with it from the start.

than to empathize or accept, but this won't help the child work through what they're going through. And we can do the same with adults—which is why when you announce you've got a cold and feel rotten, you are more likely to get advice about echinacea, vitamin C, honey and lemon, and nasal douches than the sympathy you were after, and end up feeling patronized more than comforted.

I'm not saying we are 100 percent responsible for how we feel. Of course, others impact us and we feel things in response, some of which we might not like. But what I am saying is that they are not fully responsible for how we feel either. Acknowledging a shared role in difficulties and conflict, and accepting that others may have a different way of coping from you, is the first essential step in understanding the problem and working toward a resolution.

Argument #2: It's Not Me, It's You

I have observed that many of us approach issues in our relationship as if it is the other person who has a problem and we are mere spectators. We find it more comfortable to ruminate about how other people are awful rather than look at how we are contributing to the way we're feeling. When we concentrate on the other person, it works as a deflection away from us and our feelings and needs. I think about this with regard to this next problem, from a middle-aged man who wrote me a very measured letter about his marriage.

> My wife and I are both fifty-one and have been together thirty years. She is experiencing perimenopausal symptoms and I am trying to support her as much as possible. I have always been sensitive to her needs—period pain, labor, postnatal depression, and three years of anorexia— and I have researched all I can about the perimenopause. I adore my wife and find her sexy, but I know that intimacy is not something she wants at the moment and I respect that.
>
> Our sex life has never been regular during our marriage, but I still desire her and wish for some form of intimacy when she is ready. I do not want anyone else and my outlet is self-pleasure when needed, although the teenage guilt is still there! Is there still hope for us to continue a sexual relationship when the time is right? I just don't want to accept our physical relationship could be over.

The way I see it is that this man is the one with a problem— no sex—but he views his wife as having the problem even though she appears OK with their lack of intimacy. In fact, he seems to be used to seeing his wife as a whole string of problems while not acknowledging his own. I wonder what it was about his upbringing that, at fifty-one, has left him with hang-ups about masturbation, for instance. There is also a flavor of

> ### Everyday Wisdom
>
> As we are in charge of ourselves rather than other people, if we want something to change, it is our responsibility to change ourselves. Others will respond to that change or they won't, and that is not within our control.

I-want-to-get-you-right-for-me about his attempt to fix his wife that I expect she picks up on. She may feel infantilized by him taking care of research and becoming the expert on her as if she is a specimen to be analyzed—something to be right about rather than a person to relate to—and this could be diminishing her sexual attraction toward him. It is rare that someone wants to be fixed and this approach can create distance between two people.

When trying to explain to someone how you feel about a problem, avoid telling them what you think they're like. I don't want to put words into your mouth—use your own words—but focus on how you feel around them instead and how you would like your relationship to improve. So instead of "she is irritating" or "he is not listening to me," switch to noticing "I feel irritated" or "I feel unheard," thus taking responsibility for your reactions and realizing that just because someone isn't doing what you want them to, it doesn't mean there is anything wrong with them. This habit will help you take responsibility for your response rather than blaming the other person.

It can be so much easier to see what needs fixing in someone else than it is to realize what it is in ourselves that may be limiting our relationships. We need to be aware that if we keep finding ourselves feeling the same about different groups of people, it is probably us and not them. OK, maybe it isn't you, maybe it is them, but if it's *always* them and *never* you, it's probably you. Let's look at this next example from a woman who cannot keep female friends.

> Every woman I've ever befriended since childhood ends up ghosting me.
>
> I've been wracking my brain about why these female friendships always fizzle out. I don't think I've done anything wrong that would justify ditching me. In fact, I have supported these women over the years when they've been in tricky situations. I have plenty of male friends; this ghosting only happens to me with women.
>
> I have high expectations for myself and have views about female independence, but have never commented negatively on my friends' lives. I have sought to encourage them and told them how clever, attractive, and funny they were. Could it be that they were jealous of me?
>
> I don't know what I can do differently.

As this keeps on happening, I do think it is probably her. It's a pattern: Something is going on and it is happening outside her consciousness. She isn't doing anything wrong intentionally, and if you are also in this type of situation, some detective work may be necessary. Many people, like this woman, find relationships with one sex more difficult than with those of the other. In therapy, I always ask such clients to tell me in detail how they experienced their relationship with their mother, if their problem is with women, or their father, if it is with men. Sometimes from this we can learn whether that relationship became a blueprint for subsequent interactions.

In this example, I think the woman who wrote to me could be a victim of the clichéd folklore that girls gossip, bitch, and are weak. In contrast we are fed the rumor that boys are straightforward and strong. Both girls and boys internalize these messages. Society seems to value men more: If as a girl you are said to be "one of the boys," it can be received like a compliment and make you feel superior to other girls. The way the woman who wrote to me described helping female friends didn't come across to me like it was the usual two-way exchange of mutual support. Perhaps she came across to other women as somehow saying "be like I am, have my attitude, then you'll have what I have." Other people may hear this as "don't be you, be me." Maybe she could accept men as they are, but seemed to think that women need to change? Or maybe she, automatically, unknowingly, sought out female friends to whom she could feel superior? Some internalized misogyny might be sensed by others.

Whatever it is that's happening to cause her problem, it is likely to be the result of her early environment. The good news is that while we can't change others, we do have the power to change how we react and respond, and this can change the situations we find ourselves in. We can't control other people, we can only control ourselves, and if we want to get unstuck in our relationships, we need to start by changing our actions and behaviors. It is much easier but less helpful to focus on how other people are annoying than it is to realize what it is that we're doing that's causing problems in our relationship. Once we do that, we can find a different pattern: a more helpful and loving one.

Argument #3: Goodie Versus Baddie

In the middle of an argument, it is easy to see ourselves as being the goodie and the other person as the baddie, and then we naturally select the evidence to fit. We intensify our feeling of dislike by cherry-picking the evidence that backs up our hunches and we rant to people who validate our point of view. This makes us feel right, or even self-righteous, and thus we construct a negative lens through which to view the other—making them into the bad guy. This game of "me-right, you-wrong" is something I see play out in many different situations, from parents going through a divorce to disagreements between coworkers, from couples navigating household chores to friendships that have turned sour.

It's normal human behavior to want to be right. Being wrong carries with it shame, judgment, guilt—all feelings we'd rather avoid. But this wanting to be right and thinking that we're the goodie can often lead to getting stuck in a conflict loop rather than being open to a resolution. Resentments mount up and yet you are both locked in. Neither of you is changing; neither is leaving. As someone wise once said, you can be right or you can be married, but you cannot be both. I think this applies to any type of relationship.

I recently received this letter from a young man who got into an argument with his family about an inappropriate conversation.

> During a family meal my eldest sister made a xenophobic joke. I said she was a racist and that I felt like leaving. She was angry and affronted, and denied being racist and said her joke was just a clever play on words. Although I was upset, I was persuaded to stay as I didn't want it to ruin the day, but my sister and I haven't spoken since. My mom has suggested that I take time out from family gatherings.
>
> When we were growing up we got along well, so this isn't as though it is part of an ongoing competitive dynamic or anything, but these days there are fundamental differences between me versus my mom and my sister, which I could sum up by saying, I read *The Guardian* and live in a city while they read *The Daily Mail* and live in the countryside. Despite this, we usually get

along well, and I do very much want to heal this rift, but I don't know how.

As a society we need to have one another's backs in public and most importantly in private in moments like this. Society exists, whatever Thatcher declared, and calling out bigotry when we see it counteracts hate and can help community. So well done to this man.

The joke, which I'm not going to insult anyone by repeating here, was racist. But the young man's problem isn't about whether that joke was offensive or benign. The real issue isn't that he called his sister out, it's how he did it. When we know ourselves to be right and we know that millions of people would agree with our position, it is too easy to feel self-righteous and superior. Unconsciously we may want to prove we are smarter, especially perhaps to an older sibling who traditionally may have been seen as wiser, no matter how harmonious the relationship was growing up. This man was proving his liberal credentials and fell into the trap of seeing himself and his sister through the clumsy lens of left and right politics. But we are all more complicated than that.

His journey to this point implies that at some stage he learned to think in a different way from how he was brought up, which suggests that he could understand why his sister might not get the reasons the "joke" was offensive. Rather than assuming she meant any harm or felt spiteful toward the people she was apparently mocking, perhaps she hadn't thought it through. In her bubble she might not have ever thought about how it feels to be a minority who is tired of being stereotyped, mocked, and victimized.

We need to try to see things from the other person's viewpoint. When we don't take this into consideration but just jump onto the moral high ground and label someone, that too is behavior that makes us the "goodie" and the other the "baddie." Label the joke but don't label the person. Anyone is going to be humiliated if they are labeled and called out publicly, and if we are made to feel humiliated, we are unlikely to listen to feedback and take it on board, and more likely to go into denial or try to defend ourselves. In this man's case, it was a wasted opportunity to educate, which is a shame.

Instead, I would advise him to tell them about how the joke makes him feel. He might have said something like "That's a neat play on words, but if my family was from another part of the world, it might make me feel sad, angry, or unwelcome, which is why I couldn't ever repeat it. The joke may appear almost harmless, like a small cut, but when you've had a hundred small cuts, you have a nasty wound."

Everyday Wisdom

When we feel more humble in expressing our opinion, paradoxically we may find ourselves feeling more confident rather than less, which means we won't come across as too overbearing when making our points.

He could have gone on to say, "I know you're a good person but if someone else heard you repeat that joke, they might mistake you for a racist."

Racist jokes aren't OK, attacking a sister who hadn't thought things through isn't OK, and two wrongs don't make a right. When we're feeling stuck in a conflict loop, our first job is to put aside this dynamic of one person being good and the other bad.

To illustrate this further, let's move on to this young woman who wrote to me while engaged to be married. The excitement of her impending nuptials and the idea of married life with her partner was marred by a difficult relationship with her partner's family. Her story is not unique and I regularly receive letters from people trying to navigate conflicts with their in-laws.

> My partner's mother is toxic. She tore down every decision I made regarding my wedding. We chose a dreary venue, just to appease her. My partner and I wanted to hire a food truck for an evening snack, but she responded that she "hates" foreign food. Her solution? Food by the cook at the local boarding school (the food is terrible: think dry ham sandwiches).
>
> COVID-19 meant we couldn't have our wedding as originally planned. I was thankful I wouldn't have to put up with his family. My partner now wants to get married, but I don't want to if parents are going to be present. I want to elope: I love him very much and I want to marry him. But he refuses to get married

without his parents present. His mother and sister both accused me of stealing him away from them. This hurt and I will never forgive them: I never prevented my partner from attending a family event or anything like that. He tells me I can't change them, I need to accept it and to be nice to them. Sorry, but no. No one seems to care what I, the bride, think. I feel really stuck.

When we don't feel safe in the world, we need enemies. Then we find them to try to feel in control again. That emotional charge within us seems to need people we can consider wrong, to make us feel right. Accepting others and trying to understand rather than judging them can somehow feel like you're losing out or giving in, but I promise, you're not.

This task becomes easier when we become aware of how we are interpreting the other's behavior. In the middle of an argument, take a bird's-eye view of the situation: See yourself down there, trying to fight this battle, and don't take sides. What do you notice? See if you can do this without thinking who is right and who is wrong, but just watch it unfold as you fly above it. Now that you have some distance, you can see what part you play in this scene. What does it look like? What are everyone's fears? How are they each handling them? How do they differ in what they dread? How are they similar? I expect everyone has feelings and they are handling them the only way they know how. Be curious about the feelings of others and about yours.

You might think: *Why should it be me that considers the other person's feelings? Why don't they care how I feel?* It always has to be you because you are the only one you have any control over. Their behavior may change when yours does, but there are no guarantees. It is not helpful to you to interpret everything the other person says as an attack on you because then you feel like counter-attacking. Going back to the young bride, I would suggest to her that rather than thinking *I haven't prevented him coming to any family occasion*, to instead try: *I can understand it must be frightening for his family to feel they'll see less of such a lovely man, someone so important to them. I'll try to share him.*

If you look at others' actions in a positive rather than a negative light, you can get different meanings from them. For example, another bride-to-be wrote to me with a similar issue, except that in this case, her future mother-in-law hadn't offered to help with the wedding and the young woman took that as an act of selfishness. But perhaps rather than selfishness, stepping back could be interpreted as not wanting to interfere. In other

Everyday Wisdom

Often we can fall into the trap of interpreting behavior by what it would mean if *we* did whatever the other person is doing. Someone else's behavior has a different meaning from what it would mean if you did it.

words, look for the feelings behind how others speak to you and try to empathize with those feelings.

A practical way of doing this is to take time to imagine what it is like being the other person, to have had their life and their upbringing, and appreciate the things they have made from that. Sit in a chair the way the person you are arguing with would, and try to imagine yourself in their body. How does it feel to sit like them? And then imagine you sitting with them. It can help to get into the role by saying "I am [the other person's name], I'm sitting with [your name], how do I experience my body?" Imagine what it is like to be them and how they must feel, and then feel with them.

When two people take up polarized positions, both need to exercise some give-and-take to come to a compromise. It's not always easy. Accepting people isn't always easy. But it is the only path forward.

Argument #4: Facts Versus Feelings

Conflicts are usually far more about how we each feel than they are about facts. This is at the center of how we argue and for many it requires a big shift in how they view themselves and others. There is much less logic to any of our thoughts than we'd like to believe, and logic rarely solves disputes. It is far easier to reach a solution when there is a mutual understanding of feelings. Of course, sometimes facts take precedence over feelings, but if feelings go unacknowledged, the facts are less likely to be respected. This means instead of trying to "win" using logic, try to understand by listening to feelings, yours and theirs, as this is the path to getting unstuck.

When we focus on logic rather than feelings, we can fall into a game of what I like to call fact tennis. Fact tennis is when two people in an argument are lobbing reasons and facts over the net to each other, finding more and more to hit the other person with. The aim becomes point scoring rather than finding a workable solution.

Let's take as an example this common argument when one person is taking longer to get ready to leave the house than the other. This is what happens when the process becomes fact tennis:

SERVER: It takes you ages to get ready, so if you don't start getting ready now, we'll be late going to see my parents. *15–love*

RESPONDER: That's not true, it only takes me half an hour to get ready and twenty minutes to drive there so we have time. *15 all*

SERVER: Last week it took you forty-five minutes to get ready when we went to the restaurant with my friends. *30–15*

RESPONDER: Last week I needed to wash my hair and I don't need to wash my hair this time. *30 all*

SERVER: But if we leave it too close to the wire, there might be traffic and we'll be late. We were late last time we went. *40–30*

RESPONDER: I checked the traffic report and there isn't any traffic today. *Deuce*

And on and on. Eventually one person will run out of reasons and will therefore be deemed to have "lost." Though the argument is superficially resolved, they may continue to feel annoyed and resentful. And if the "winner" feels good, it will be at the expense of their partner.

If we put logic to the side and instead focus on feelings, the same conversation is more likely to go like this:

1ST PERSON: I get anxious when we leave it too close to the wire to leave the house to see my parents. I know it irritates my dad when people are late and it puts him in a bad mood.

2ND PERSON: Oh, sorry, darling, I don't like you to feel anxious and I can see that being late to see your parents isn't nice for them. I want to finish this piece of work so that I can be present with your family later.

1ST PERSON: Yeah, you do have a lot going on. How about I help by ironing your dress so that it's ready when you're done, and you can get ready more quickly?

Listening to differences and working through them is about understanding and compromise, not about winning. Rather than damning others with judgments, I think our lives would be better if we remained open with curiosity. For the best outcome, aim for understanding and empathy rather than judgment and victory. It is much better if we can think of differences, not so much as I'm right, they're wrong, winning and losing, but as an opportunity to gain an understanding of

> **Everyday Wisdom**
>
> Trying to "win" arguments through facts and logic is unhelpful and pushes everyone into a harmful game of right and wrong. Instead of judgment and victory, try to build understanding and empathy.

the other's viewpoint and to communicate how we feel about ours. Put aside rights and wrongs, don't seek to blame and/or get an apology, but try instead to understand. Being right is overrated.

Argument #5: The Karpman Drama Triangle

Many counselors use something called the Karpman Drama Triangle to make sense of what is happening in a relationship. The point of it is to put to one side what you are arguing about and examine instead your patterns of relating to one another. Imagine a triangle: the pointy bit at the bottom is labeled Victim, and the other two corners are labeled Persecutor and Rescuer.

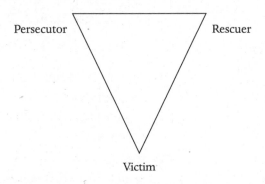

The point of the Karpman Drama Triangle is to get to the root of the conflict and realize that arguments are often less about the actual issue being discussed and more about the ways that we feel we are being treated by the other person. This is why arguments about the smallest, most seemingly insignificant things can end up turning into heated situations.

To illustrate the triangle in action, let us look at the following story. This person's partner suffers from depression but refuses to seek help or take her medication. Frustrated and desperate, the husband wrote to me.

> My wife has suffered from depression for decades but only saw the doctor once, stopped taking the medication after a few months, and refuses to go on it again.

She won't talk to anyone or seek help professionally or from family—not even me.

In the last two years, COVID-19 has had a major impact on her mental health, and her behavior on top of this is now affecting me massively. In the past, I've been told I'm very positive and happy. I'm certainly not that now.

I try hard to get things right, and I'm not perfect—but nothing I do is good enough for her. She talks at me as though I'm stupid. It is not in my nature to be aggressive, but sometimes I have to defend myself. I'm being constantly made to feel guilty that everything is my fault.

She doesn't have any close friends or any hobbies, and she seems to resent me when I do things, but she won't do them with me.

At the moment, they are both dancing around the triangle from Rescuer to Persecutor to Victim and back again. The man who wrote to me is getting into the Rescuer role by trying to persuade his wife to get help for her depression. She then experiences this as persecution and gets defensive and persecutes him, and then he feels like the Victim. This is a common

> **Everyday Wisdom**
>
> Be mindful of the language you use with others. A good way to start is to speak in "I" statements, which define your own experience, and not "You" statements, which are a judgment on the other person.

cycle that many people—couples, family members, friends—fall into when disagreeing.

So, how to escape from these three unhelpful roles? We can change how we react to others and see what happens, or we can leave. If we choose the former, firstly we have to learn how not to persecute: We can ban ourselves from using certain phrases, such as "You always...," "You are...," "You should..." In other words, we can speak in "I" statements, which define our own experience, and not "You" statements. Avoid using words like "should." Say how something makes you feel, and then say what behavior you would like instead. This habit will help you take responsibility for your response rather than blaming the other person and will lead to a conversation that is less combative.

How we say things is just as important as what we're saying. Defer judging altogether and be curious about people, and yourself, instead. It's not necessary to damn anyone or praise them, you can just be interested in them. Don't define them and don't give unasked-for advice, because these types of remarks are likely to be experienced as persecutory, however well intended the sentiment behind them is. If you can say what is bothering you in a nonjudgmental way, then other people can hear you, not take it as an attack, and you can work together toward a solution without escalating the situation.

Secondly, when we are trying too hard to get things right for others, that's when we are in the Rescuer role.

We get into rescue mode when we do things for people that they are capable of doing for themselves. They might experience this as infantilizing, shutting them down and pushing them away rather than pulling them close. I see this behavior particularly in men. In our culture, we big-up men and boys to be knights in shining armor and downplay girls and women into damsels in distress, so it's too easy to take it for granted that it's the male role to problem solve. But it isn't. Don't try to be perfect; being you is enough.

Thirdly, when you play the victim, you are giving away your power. Recognize when you are playing the martyr and stop. If you allow yourself to be dragged down by someone else, you will resent them for it. If you don't allow it, you won't. And you know what they say about resentment? "Resentment is like drinking poison and expecting your enemy to die." Real victims are helpless and cannot take responsibility for their predicament. Playing the victim is different—you are choosing not to take responsibility.

Even when someone else belittles you, you don't have to play the victim to their persecution. When I'm insulted, I can use the following way of diffusing the situation instead of getting aggressive. For example, in response to the insult "You're stupid," I could say, "Oh, you think I'm stupid, thanks for letting me know." In other words, I don't agree or disagree with what's been said, but I show them I've heard. Echoing back what you've heard so you don't ignore them will calm things down. I also feel by repeating it to them I am somehow giving it back to them. I think this is because then I can feel that their statement is about them and not necessarily about me.

Acknowledging others' feelings, no matter how uncomfortable they might make us feel, is an important step toward working out where the differences are. Rather than going against someone, go in the same direction and put their actions and behavior into words. When we feel heard we don't have to shout louder. Going back to our example, if the wife says something like "Doctors can't help me," the husband doesn't have to argue. Immediately contradicting her is likely to get them both fired up with little chances of resolution. Instead, he can respond with "Ah, you feel doctors can't help you." They will be going in the same direction, feeling seen and understood, and they can begin to brainstorm solutions. After they've both agreed that she believes doctors can't help, he might say, "I would be so much less anxious if you gave the doctors another try." This will be experienced by his wife differently from the more combative "You should . . . ," because he would be defining his own self and taking responsibility for his response rather than placing blame on his wife. When a step is taken to be more vulnerable and open in a relationship, the other person often follows suit.

Argument #6: Conflict Avoidant

Compromise isn't about agreeing with others com-pletely. That leads to resentment and disconnect. If conflict is completely avoided, not talked about, and never aired, a relationship can shrink because, as subjects become taboo, it means there will be less and less to talk about and areas of loneliness creep in where each person remains unseen. Unless we air the differences we have with each other, then the relationship just disappears. I'm not saying that some conflict shouldn't be let go—if you have a resentment or a grudge, it's best to let it go—but take the example of a married couple. If the woman just bottles up everything her husband does and says to her and suppresses her feelings, it might be a peaceful house but eventually she'll feel isolated and unheard. A fear of arguing can lead to less intimacy and may leave you bit-ter, not better. Part of this work involves setting boundaries like those discussed in Chapter 1, but another crucial element is allowing yourself to feel your emo-tions fully, even if not necessarily acting on them.

Let's look at this next example of a man who wrote to me after discovering his wife had been having an affair.

> My six-year marriage came to an end after my ex-wife started an affair. At couples counseling I learned that when our eldest started school, my wife began getting

attention from a few of the school dads. This excited her but also made her aware that she couldn't reciprocate because she was in a monogamous relationship. She began to resent me and our marriage—it wasn't so much that she wanted another relationship, more that she wanted to experience the heady rush of a new relationship. She became infatuated with one particular dad and they began an affair. We had both couples and individual counseling. My ex soon felt "judged" and stopped attending. When I became upset about our marriage falling apart, she said she sympathized but then told me I was just using "emotional blackmail."

We've kept things civil for the sake of the kids. I don't want to be a bitter ex. But I have a lot of withheld anger—her behavior and actions caused so much trauma, not just to me, but to her now-partner's ex, her parents, our kids, and friends. But I suppress it and even feel guilty about feeling it. My counselor has challenged me on this and has even said: "All we hear is how you're understanding, but why aren't you angry?" My ex says she must live her truth and be true to her feelings, that she tried her hardest and she's only human.

The anger I feel is essentially a tantrum at not having things my own way. And that thought appalls me, so I suppress it. How do you deal with unresolved anger that you feel guilty about feeling, let alone show it?

For many people, including this man, anger equals "bad." We often associate it with "tantrums," which is equating anger with childishness, lack of impulse control, or overentitlement. Many of us, when shouted at, experience fear. We don't listen to the words being yelled at us, we only notice that they are loud and alarming. We have feelings of shock and adrenaline as if we have been subjected to physical rather than just verbal violence. No one feels safe if they are shouted at and therefore cannot open up to talk. And it is very natural when you feel you are attacked to attack back.

Anger has got a bad press. But it isn't the feeling that is bad. It is the behavior that sometimes goes with that feeling that can be destructive or frightening. Quite often adults make children feel they are wrong to be angry, or sad, or have any negative emotions. What the adults really object to is the behavior children display when they are angry: the shouting, the hitting, the sulking. Babies and toddlers, as anyone who has lived in close proximity to one will know, are not always terribly good at articulating what they feel, but they are very good at acting out their emotions: they bite, they scream, they lie on the floor and beat their fists, and generally try to squirm out of situations that don't appeal to them. We don't dispute that when a baby throws his toys out of the stroller, he is actually doing his best to show how he feels.

Sometimes how a child feels is inconvenient for us, but we must not be tempted to argue with what they feel or declare that they are silly for feeling it. Because we want our children to be happy, they can feel they are disappointing us if they are not. This means it's harder for them to talk to us if they believe they won't be taken seriously. Our rush to regain equilibrium might make them feel unacceptable if they have uncomfortable emotions or weird thoughts and that they have no space to work them out. If we invalidate their feelings and thus teach them to overrule such feelings, we are endangering them. I'm not saying we shouldn't contain their feelings or comfort them, nor am I saying our actions should be dictated by what they feel, but I am saying that we need to acknowledge them and take them seriously. Validation also teaches children to be able to empathize with others' subjective experience too, thus learning to accept that how one person feels may be different from how another does.

If this does not happen to a child, they can grow up not knowing how to express what they're feeling because they have been taught—like the man in the aforementioned example seems to have been taught—that they are unacceptable and childish for having that feeling. Had this man been helped to find acceptable ways of expressing his anger while growing up, he wouldn't be in the position of not knowing what to do with his feelings now.

If we haven't been shown how to deal with anger, it's never too late to start. The idea is not to act out the anger by screaming or lashing out at the person or thing that's made you angry, but instead putting the anger into words. Putting a feeling into words is what we call in therapy "processing feelings." When you can calmly talk about how you feel, you have control of the feeling rather than the feeling having control of you. If we don't get into the habit of doing this, we will continue to act out the feeling, or hold it in, where it might burn away at us.

When there is an electrical charge of anger, it's usually rooted in the past and not the present. Having an awareness of this is part of respecting your feelings in any situation of conflict. Perhaps you get furious when someone tells you you're wrong, and that anger is a reaction built up from all the times you were patronized or gaslit in the past, not only to that one instance. In the example, this man has his anger in a metaphorical box and is firmly sitting on the lid. Maybe he fears if he took the lid off it would explode. But it doesn't feel great—it sounds as if it's eating him up inside—and it isn't sustainable. He is going to have to help himself by letting it out a bit at a time.

Anger management means being able to express anger as well as control it. Many of us learn to numb emotion because having feelings often means having pain at some point. Trouble is, we cannot just numb hurt and pain without numbing joy as well. Sit on one feeling and you'll be sitting on them all. It's OK to be upset when you don't get your own way. You are entitled to feel anger, but you are not entitled to hurt anyone with it. But that doesn't mean you need to let that anger stay inside where it is hurting you. There is no need to add guilt to your anger by telling yourself that you have no right to be angry. That will only add to your burden.

If you're angry at a situation or at a person and you feel unable to speak calmly about it, get a cushion to hit or scream into and really scream. Shout! You may need to scream and shout in a safe place with an empathetic, encouraging witness. I went into a field and yelled at an innocent tree once: The tree didn't mind, and it really helped. You can also write a letter about why you're so angry. List every injustice, say why it's unfair, say why it's not your fault, say how furious you are, but don't post it. Burn it and watch the embers float away. You might have to write another one every day for a month, but it's good to process feelings into words. Try a boxing gym and let that punching bag have it. Have a tantrum in a safe space, then have another one; it's OK, you will control it, and you can let it out a bit at a time.

It is only when you have given yourself the space to feel the full extent of your feelings that you can calmly describe to others how and why you are angry and open yourself up to seeing things from another point of view. This man was as entitled to express how angry he was as his ex-wife believed herself entitled to her feelings. I hope I convinced him that anger is not childish and that we can express it in a non-frightening yet assertive way.

Argument #7: When Impulse Takes Over

We can get very good at processing and managing our feelings, but sometimes impulse takes over and we act in ways we regret or say things we don't mean to. My youngest correspondent so far has been a nine-year-old boy, who wrote to me alongside his mother. I really liked the way they both wrote to me and that she didn't go behind his back. That required honesty and openness.

A while back my son physically hurt a friend at school. He stopped when the teacher scolded him. The friend has moved on, forgiven him, and even invited him to his birthday party, but it is haunting my son as he still feels bad and really anxious about it. What happened was very much out of character and he can't explain why he did it.

Here is my son's letter to you: I am a nine-year-old boy. A couple of months ago, I hurt my friend by squeezing his neck tight. I don't know why. Maybe I was overtired. Now I deeply regret this and have been feeling guilty almost every day since. I apologized and I keep apologizing. The boy I hurt forgave me quickly, but I can't seem to forgive myself. What doesn't help is that I'm not religious so I can't speak to God and ask him for forgiveness. After it happened, I was so distressed and quiet, but those feelings were bottled up inside me. Sometimes when I think about it my stomach hurts. I'm writing in the hope you'll teach me how to move on.

Yes, an all-powerful God, with powers of forgiveness, would make things simple, but many of us are not religious, so we need more ideas. What I told him, and what I tell many others who come to me with similar problems, is that no one is good all the time. Shame and guilt are uncomfortable but quite good feelings because they remind us not to do it again. Sometimes we experiment, the experiment is a disaster, and we learn that isn't a good way of going about things.

Although we only have one brain, we could be thought of as having two: an animal brain and a reasoning brain. In emergencies, like when you step into the road without looking, it is our animal brain that makes us jump back onto the pavement before the bus hits us. We need our animal brain as sometimes we need to act before we can think. When we are babies and children, we are almost all animal brain, and then, as we grow up, we learn when to be in animal mode and when to be in reasoning mode. Sometimes our animal brain gets the better of us. It gets confused about when we need instant emergency action to survive and when we need to have a more thought-out response. Children are allowed to make these mistakes. Mistakes help us to learn. That's why, when we are younger, we have adults looking after us because they expect us to have lapses. This boy and his friend were OK because there was a teacher to say stop and, when they did, he stopped. He instantly knew—when the teacher reminded him—that he didn't have to hurt his friend. I call that winning. I'm not worried for this boy: I think his teacher and mom will continue to help him learn when it's not appropriate for the animal brain to take charge and when it is.

When the boy says he was "overtired," I suspect this reason came from an adult. Adults love that explanation when something more complicated may have been going on. Was he being teased? Or maybe he felt under pressure and the only way he could express it or find release in the moment was by applying similar pressure to his friend's neck. A good idea is to put feelings into words before they begin to feel like an emergency to our animal brain. It can be difficult, but talking releases pressure.

Everyday Wisdom

We don't have to have it all worked out before we start to talk—sometimes we only find out what we are feeling, or what we know, in conversation with others.

What this boy's story also shows is that it can be very difficult to forgive ourselves when we do something we later regret. We are human, and humans make mistakes and that's how we learn. Even adults go inappropriately into animal brain sometimes. Learning to control impulsivity does not come naturally to everyone. The key is to concentrate on developing the skills needed in the following areas: tolerating frustration, flexibility, problem-solving, and learning to see and feel things from other people's points of view. Some people naturally pick up these skills as they grow up and others need to learn them in adulthood. Learning how to reflect and then respond, rather than just reacting, is a slow process requiring practice and patience and sometimes professional help too. Just like building new muscles in the gym takes time so does building the necessary new pathways in your brain.

If you notice yourself worrying and fretting after an argument, don't give yourself up to the worrying, but keep a part of yourself back to watch yourself worrying. The part of you that's keeping watch—that's your reasoning brain—can tell the worrying part of you that it's OK to fret and feel guilty if you want to, but you don't need to. And it's OK to have a cry and/or a shout and let those feelings out (to a tree or to an understanding person who has given their consent).

Aim for Assertive

There's a reason the phrase "it's not what you say, it's how you say it" is commonly used, and that's because it is a well-observed phenomenon. The wonderful thing about being considerate of how you communicate is that it is something within your power. You are not in control of how people act or behave, but you are in control of how you choose to talk to them about it.

The question of how to strike a balance between too strict and combative or too easygoing and lax is something that comes up particularly when it concerns professional conversations and relationships. There is a difference between taking responsibility for your response and being aware of your role in the dynamic, and becoming a people-pleaser. Let's look at this example of a female conflict-phobic CEO.

I need help with my career. My heart sinks every morning—I feel overwhelmed, under-capable. Everything is a firefight and I just get through and think OK, and then I must face it all again the next day, repeat ad nauseam.

I feel I'm overpromoted. Probably because of a family connection. I run a large organization. I feel like a fraud and I have no idea how to make people do things; I just am not a natural leader in this area. I want to "like" people into doing things. I never "command"; I always almost plead—a sort of "Please, please, if you could would you..." puppy-dog style. And it is exhausting. I am not strategically bad—on that level I think I am OK—but it is all the rest.

I spend half my time worrying whether I have upset someone, said something wrong, or been misunderstood and whether I can get this or that person to like me. It is all so exhausting. I suppose this has been my philosophy throughout life. I don't think it is a good strategy for life either, but I don't seem to have an alternative. I feel as if I have never quite grown up. I tried executive coaching, but it didn't work.

If we overdo the people-pleasing it probably has the opposite effect of what we would wish because it can be annoying to be over-flattered. When we bend over backward to get it right for the other, we often lose our ground and wisdom in the process. However, someone who doesn't or who can't consider another's feelings or thoughts is not great either.

A simple way to find that space between commanding and pleading is to think about how you would like to be asked to do something. You wouldn't want to be asked in such a wishy-washy way that meant you didn't know whether it was important or not. Nor would you like to be commanded as though you were some sort of robot or slave with no choice or brain of your own. Experiment with more direct communication. To do this, again stick to "I" statements. So rather than say "You are always late to meetings," try "We can lose clients if you keep them waiting. I need you to be five minutes early to these meetings." The general rule being, state the consequence of their behavior, and then say what behavior you would like instead.

If you need something done by someone, give them a bit of choice but not too much. This is useful outside work too. We get better results if we say to an employee "We need to talk about this before the end of the day. Is it better to talk in person or over the phone?" rather than if we tell them "I'll be talking about this to you," or pleading with them to "maybe have a chat when you have a second." We aren't putting into question whether the conversation will be happening, but we are giving them the choice of how it does so that they are more comfortable.

The trouble with being a woman is that we are often trained by our background and culture to be more likeable than assertive. The first way this shows up is how we talk about ourselves, to ourselves, and to others. Returning to our example, being assertive means changing phrases like "I am not strategically bad—on that level I think I am OK—but it is all the rest" to "My strength is being able to strategize." When you've practiced the middle way between commanding and pleading, you will feel more like an adult. If, like the writer of my letter, you struggle with impostor syndrome, this will help diminish it. Aiming for mutual respect with others rather than just being liked will also make you, and them, feel better. The best leaders are not those who dominate, but those who listen, respect, and consider feedback from others when deciding.

Just like all the other pieces of advice in this chapter—make everything into an "I" statement rather than a "You" statement, avoid words like "should" and "must," look past the "I'm right and you're wrong" game—much of what is applicable when navigating conflict with your coworkers will be applicable to how you talk to your mother-in-law or spouse, best friend or grandchild. People are people after all. And learning to be assertive will help in all areas of your life.

Over and Out

Up until now, this chapter has been about helping relationships get through tricky moments. But sometimes it's not worth resolving the conflict as the relationship is not worth saving, and you're better off exiting left, followed by a bear. Cutting ties is rarely as destructive as many of us imagine and might be the best path forward (unless it's your habit to always cut ties, and then you could consider looking at that pattern). Most of us know this with regard to breaking up with a romantic partner, but I do think it's important to remember that breaking up is not only limited to romantic relationships—we can prioritize our own happiness in any relationship, even if that means ending it. You may disappoint the other person, but irreconcilable differences may mean your relationship cannot continue. Not everyone is meant to be in our life forever and it is OK to acknowledge and act on that.

I think about this with regard to the next story from a young woman who was asked by a friend to be her bridesmaid.

> She's been engaged for five years. The whole thing has had to be rescheduled twice due to the pandemic and now it's taking place next year.
>
> When she became engaged, I was one of her only friends. We had been teenage friends and used to go out drinking and partying. She started working and became sensible and ambitious, met her fiancé, and settled down. I went to college, met a bunch of people I bonded with, and we started to drift apart. She asked me to be her bridesmaid more than four years ago and I think it was because at that time there were not many other people she could ask.

Since then, our friendship has continued to diminish. She refuses ever to meet on weeknights because of work and doesn't like to go out on the weekend anymore. I go to her house for a cup of tea about twice a year. She talks wedding plans, we do a rudimentary catching up, and then I leave. We don't speak for months at a time. We don't share any interests; we don't have any other friends in common. I haven't even met her fiancé. Neither of us has really put any time or effort into our friendship. Unfortunately, she cares strongly about the perfect wedding, another thing that we don't agree on. My dilemma is this: I am working a low-pay job and cannot afford a four-day bachelorette party abroad. I want to get out of this responsibility. I do not want to go to the bachelorette party, be a bridesmaid, or even go to the wedding. My friends tell me to grin and bear it, that it's only a few days, but I have never wanted to escape a situation more.

We have all had those people in our life who only want to spend time with us on their terms—at the times and locations that suit them. They don't match the effort we put into the relationship and yet expect us to continue to go above and beyond for them. In this case, our heroine is expected to make good on her promise to be the perfect bridesmaid, which tarnishes her life with background dread. If she gets herself out of this situation, she will get back more than saved money and a few days: She'll also free herself from months of this trepidation. It will be horrible to be the "bad person" and the extraction process will be unpleasant, but the relief of not having to go through this charade will make up for that.

If I were her, this is the note I would write to the bride-to-be:

> Dear X, I am really sorry, I know I promised all those years ago to be your bridesmaid and a good person would keep good her promise. But as your wedding approaches I find myself not wanting to be a bridesmaid, not wanting to join the bachelorette party, and not even really wanting to go to the wedding. I realize by extracting myself I'm not being a great friend to you and I'm sorry. It's not just that I can't afford it and I can't, it's that I don't want to be there. I can't put on an act and I don't want to spoil your day by not being enthusiastic. I hope you have a wonderful day and I'm sorry. Love from Y.

It can be hard to believe that someone who used to be important to us is now someone we have far less in common with, but this is what can happen. If you need permission to cut someone out of your life because they fill it with dread, I am giving it to you. You don't need excuses, your dread is reason enough. There is a

---

Everyday Wisdom

Sometimes being authentic means we're not as kind as we would wish to be. If this makes you feel guilty, remember that guilt is better than resentment.

---

strong possibility they'll not see it like that and be very hurt. But one of you will suffer—either you with the dread, or them with the hurt. Free yourself and release whoever it is that is causing you this dread from having a hostage in their life.

Rupture and Repair

If you feel betrayed or your trust has been broken, it can be difficult to forgive the person who has hurt you and to let go of the resentment that has built up as a consequence. The next story is an example of this. The woman who wrote to me has been married to her husband for forty years but was shocked to discover he had been having a thirty-year affair.

> I picked up his phone thinking it was mine and I noticed a text from an unknown woman. He'd been texting, making arrangements, all in affectionate and loving language. When I challenged him he told me they'd had an affair lasting five years about thirty years ago. He said the guilt made him break it off, even though she was distraught. He swears he never wanted to leave me. They resumed contact although as a friendship rather than a sexual relationship.
>
> He would visit her, but he denies anything physical happened and insists neither of them wanted to jeopardize our marriage. I'm devastated. I've seen a side of him

I've never known. He is adamant it was just friendship, but texts included him telling her he loved her, which he hasn't said to me for years.

Our marriage has involved no physical touch for a long time. I've always believed he just isn't a physically affectionate person, but even during the raw trauma of the last weeks, he hasn't hugged me. I've told him I find touch comforting, but it seems impossible.

I feel that their relationship has taken so much away from ours. He agrees and has been apologetic. We're in our early seventies with children and grandchildren. The thought of ending the marriage and stressing our family seems destructive. We've agreed to try to repair things, but part of me wonders if I'm crazy to stay with someone who has been unfaithful, sexually and emotionally, for so long. I am in shock. Am I being stupid, weak, pathetic? Can couples recover from situations like this?

It's important to note that her question to me wasn't if they should end it, but rather if it is possible for them to recover. First of all, I want to make clear that she isn't being stupid, weak, or pathetic. And yes, some couples do recover from situations like theirs, but it can feel like climbing Everest. Sometimes the betrayed partner suffers post-traumatic stress disorder as their emotional well-being has been threatened and sense of safety compromised.

It would be hard to draw a line under such an affair without working through everything—and probably with a couples therapist. As the one betrayed, this woman will need to work through the trauma of the affair and all the times she doubted her instincts and sense of reality. She will need a lot of time for this part of the process while, for her husband, it will be something that won't be able to happen quickly enough. But it will be important that they both stay with it. They could ring-fence discussions, ensuring they only happen during counseling and at other set times, so it does not overwhelm them and they both have structure and support for these necessary conversations.

When two people in a relationship—whether that's a romantic partnership, a friendship, or close family members—experience a moment of rupture, it's likely that they will have to learn new ways of communicating and of being together if they are to repair what's been broken. They will probably have to find new ways to deal with conflict and ways of building trust. Most importantly they will need to be proactive about being open and sharing emotions, including anger, and desires and thoughts, to allow a new closeness and warmth to build. They will need to find ways to switch their focus away from what is wrong in their relationship to what is right— those scraps of love. They will need to get into the habit of these loving behaviors before they begin to address any complaints to reestablish trust. And it is amazing that when we decide to act in loving, forgiving ways, it can make us feel more loving too. Feelings follow behavior. It will take practice. Intimate conversation leads to being on the same page emotionally, which is the foundation for any relationship.

It can be equally hard to be the person who is on the receiving end of a rupture. This next letter is from a man who moved abroad and is now estranged from his daughter.

> I am a sixty-eight-year-old divorced man. Fifteen years ago, I left the UK for a life abroad. My daughter was twenty-one at the time, had left college, and was living in a shared house near where her mother lived. It was the right move for me and brought me a lot of success in my professional life. I started several flourishing businesses and an international charity that I now run. My personal life has also blossomed since leaving the UK and I have remarried.
>
> When I moved away, my daughter and I were not getting along particularly well because she had ganged up with her mother against me. I was depressed because life in the UK wasn't working for me, and her mother also had mental health difficulties that meant that she was sometimes not available for our daughter. So instead of letting her know when I first made up my mind to move, I announced it to her the week before leaving, with everything already packed and sorted. I look back now and bitterly regret how I told her. I am sorry to say that we never made up and this is the big regret of my life.

I think the reason for the estrangement was not that I moved abroad, but that I hadn't told her earlier. I handled it badly for her and for myself with terrible consequences. I can guess she may have felt abandoned by me, but she never answered when I called, so I don't know.

I do love my life now, but I regret not having my daughter in it. I love her intensely. I do not know how to approach the estrangement and it is eating into me. I feel she has erased me. My partner thinks I should try to get back in touch, but I have no idea how, and with each year that passes it feels more impossible.

It is so sad that this man doesn't see his daughter. Despite his successful life, it is obviously a deep loss for him that they are still not speaking.

There isn't one particular style of communication or a specific type of conflict that leads to estrangement. In cases of rupture, the different parties will often believe it was caused by completely different reasons. For instance, parents usually report that the cause must have been the divorce or unfair accusations made about them by their ex-partner, but the adult children usually cite mistreatment like abuse, neglect, or feeling unseen, unaccepted, or unimportant to their parents.

Although this man's daughter might not have liked the way the move was announced (perhaps she would have preferred knowing his process as it happened, or maybe she wanted him to be more interested in her and her life), it is unlikely to be the cause of her wanting nothing to do with him now. Since estrangement usually happens after an event, like the announcement of a divorce—or in this man's case the announcement of a move abroad—we tend to think it is that incident that caused the rupture, but a single incident is rarely the main cause. It is usually an accumulation of things, and how the other person has experienced, interpreted, and perceived those things.

If I were in this man's situation—or in any situation where people I love have decided to break their relationship with me—I would write or talk to my daughter of my sadness about the estrangement. I would say that I wanted to try to understand it from her point of view, and would ask for her help in understanding what her experience had been and how she interpreted that experience. If she replied I would attempt to see all the events and feelings that led her to this point. I would then say back to her what she had told me, just to be certain that she knows I have listened and have not been defensive. Any defensiveness would reignite her anger and that would not be in this man's best interests.

Being right is not the best way to repair a rupture. The best way is to listen, understand, and show that you have understood. When the person you are trying to reconnect with feels understood, then—and only then, and only if they want to know—I would say what my experience has been. What my regrets were and what I don't regret. Whether they responded to my overtures or not, I would assure them that they are always in my thoughts.

If I was likely to die first and they were very important to me, like this man's daughter obviously is to him, I would leave them an account of my life, money, and a keepsake in my will.

Where there has been a rupture in a relationship, it is never too late to attempt a repair. No action could come with any guarantee, but we can try. We can open the door. Nothing might happen. But it is more likely not to happen if we stay behind a closed door.

There are as many arguing styles as there are people. The case studies in this chapter aren't meant to be taken as templates because every relationship is different and so is every argument.

However, I hope that by identifying some common patterns of how we argue, it helps you to recognize whether the way you communicate and relate to others is working for you or not. If it isn't, I hope this chapter has given you some ideas for how you might change your approach. The goal isn't to avoid arguing or to win every argument: the goal is to make progress, reach mutual understanding and compromise, and ultimately have stronger and authentic relationships.

3.   How We Change

Navigating the New, for Better or Worse

We may kid ourselves with our routines that life can stand still, or that there is such a thing as "forever," but in reality, there is only one constant in life and that is change. Babies become children, who become adults, who become old, and then life ends. No matter what winding trajectory your life takes, change is the one universal rule that makes no exceptions.

A mentally healthy person is someone who accepts this and adapts accordingly to the flux of their lives and the lives of those around them. But this doesn't make change something that is always easy to accept or simple to enact. Sometimes we dread change and cannot stop it happening, and sometimes we long for it but don't know how to bring it about. Perhaps we feel stuck in our life, or we might want to break old habits and build new ones.

This chapter is aimed at helping you look change in the eye and understand what your attitude toward it is. It may help you in discovering if and where you want your approach to change and give you some suggestions for how to put that into practice. Above all, I hope it gives you confidence and reassurance in coping with the new and unknown.

How to Get Unstuck

I receive plenty of emails about how badly other people behave and how terrible that makes our lives, and asking what we can do to solve those terrible other people. My answer is often disappointing for those who write to me because I respond that if we want things to change, we have to start with ourselves. We have to bring a certain amount of self-awareness to how we are making ourselves feel and behave as we do.

A good example of this is to take a moment to notice your breath. When you become aware of how you are breathing, you will probably slow your breathing down, and when you slow your breathing down, you are likely to feel calmer. This principle applies to a lot more than your breath. You can't make any change until you are aware of how you organize your body, your thoughts, your belief systems, and how you impact others and relate to them. It takes time, thought, and practice to make a breakthrough that will improve your life.

When we wish for something to be different, we tend to want that change to be outside ourselves—to be in the form of a savior, such as a Prince Charming, or to win the lottery, or for our significant other to undergo a character transformation. And this is normal. But just because passivity is normal, it doesn't mean it's viable. I received this letter from a man who feels stuck in the past, obsessed with an old flame, and unable to move forward. He finds it easier to blame others for how he feels instead of being curious about his own role in those feelings.

Forty years ago, as I was leaving school and starting college, I had an all-consuming relationship with a young woman. She ended it in a long, drawn-out way, which left me a wreck. I had a breakdown, which went pretty much unacknowledged by everyone. I staggered through my studies and then life carried on although the trauma of losing her never left me. I lost what promised to be a good academic career and have always been haunted by "what might have been." Incidentally my lost love went on to have a brilliant academic career. I have been in and out of therapy with depression for decades.

Thirty years ago, I met the woman who I am now married to. We have been together very happily and have two wonderful children—she is a great mother. A year ago, my lost love made contact, which prompted an immense crisis for me. I have maintained contact, but we've not met up. However, this has allowed me to deal with the forty-year-old issues, and I'm now in a much happier place.

My wife, on the other hand, is convinced she is second-best. I have promised to let her know whenever there is contact by text or email, which I have done, although every instance is difficult. She is upset by any contact, and I feel she is spying on me. I rarely initiate the contact myself. My old lover has shown no inclination to take things any further; she's single and adamant that she doesn't want to be a seductress. I want to maintain a friendship; she is the only person I still know from that period of my life. Dealing with the past trauma and forming a new relationship with her has been extremely good for me. But my wife's reactions are unbearable. If I broke things off, I will once again lose someone I am still fond of.

If I were this man's wife, I would not be reassured by him thinking of his friend from the past as his "lost love." But that aside, it sounds like he is not taking responsibility for where he is in his life or for any of his actions. He seems to be blaming those around him for how he feels and for what happens to him as though he is someone to whom things just happen. The only reassurance he has that he isn't going to resume his affair is that *she* doesn't want to be seen as a seductress. It is as though he sees himself without agency. He needs to ask himself how he got to this place in his life rather than view himself as a beach ball thrown between his old girlfriend and his wife.

When people are stuck, often I find they don't know they have a choice about how they respond to their world. Life simply appears to happen to them without them having to take responsibility for their actions or inaction, and for the subsequent consequences. It is like they are stuck in the back seat of their life, unhappy that the driver isn't taking them to where they want to go. It's true that sometimes great things do just happen: People do win the lottery (if they buy a ticket) or happen to be in the right place at the right time. Some things are down to luck—like being born in a first world country or receiving a first-rate education—but although luck undoubtedly helps, we cannot depend on luck alone.

Certain experiences can cause us to develop a victim mentality. This can then seem to be part of our identity, but it is an adaption to our environment, and it can be changed. Past experiences can make us so hypervigilant that we begin to assume every situation is about us, and this reinforces our negative view of others and our life.

One of the indicators of victim mode is giving a list of reasons why any solution offered to us will not work, so people who try to help are left confused or frustrated. There are no advantages to being a victim, but there are to being stuck in victim mode, such as not having to take responsibility for things that happen in our lives and blaming everything bad on other people's actions. In these moments, we can remember that, although we are not responsible for other people's behavior, we are responsible for how we react to them. We can change our responses, our priorities, our belief systems. I think about the Austrian psychiatrist Viktor Frankl, who was in a concentration camp during World War II. Even at his most powerless, he realized he had power over his own mind and where he directed it to go. He had power to find meaning in his life, to control what thoughts he allowed in, rather than letting his captors invade his brain.

If we merely blame other people for how we feel or for what happened in our life, if we keep blaming bad luck, it means that we don't confront what we are doing to keep ourselves stuck and we remain closed to what we could do to get unstuck. We have to keep learning, adapting, and working with the ebb and flow of life's circumstances rather than being disappointed when immovable objects don't bend to us. As the motivational speaker Ed Foreman says: "If we always do what we've always done, then we're going to get what we've always got." We get into these habits, and they take awareness and willpower to shift.

> **Everyday Wisdom**
>
> The short answer to how we get unstuck is to take responsibility for our actions and belief systems. Identify your patterns of behavior, notice whether these are a response to the past, and then start to respond to your circumstances as they are now.

We all build up patterns of behavior in response to our earliest environment. Unconsciously we might come up with some good strategies that help us survive or even thrive in those environments—but those defenses can become outdated when we move on in life, like from home to school, or from college to work. For example, you might have survived your childhood by keeping quiet and out of sight because you learned early on that this was the way you avoided being hit or shouted at. Now this strategy of lying low and saying little might hinder you in getting noticed at work, might not get you that promotion you want, and it's not the best strategy for finding friends or getting a partner. Or perhaps your early defense mechanism was to make a joke of everything because it made you popular and protected your real feelings. There's a time and a place for jokes, but if it's your only way of communicating, there will be aspects of relationships that you'll miss out on.

The first step to getting unstuck is to gain greater awareness of what those patterns are that are keeping us stuck. They can be difficult to pinpoint as they become a part of us, and we might not even realize we rely on them, but we do need to change them in order to grow and adapt to life as it unfolds. If we're lucky, we might have good friends who can kindly point them out to us. Once we've identified those patterns, we can start to respond to our present as it *is* rather than how we might respond to it if it were in the past.

Going back to the man who wrote to me, I think it's time he thought about how his patterns and habits are contributing to his own stuckness. He needs to challenge his victim mindset and break free from that inner hurt, lovesick, unrealistic teenage boy who has been holding him prisoner for what sounds like the past forty years. The only person who can release him from that prison is himself. He can stop being a beach ball thrown between his "lost love" and his wife, and decide instead what he wants for himself. Whether it's to be with his wife, with his "lost love," or with neither, he can put himself in the driver's seat and head in that direction. The disadvantage of this, of course, is that he has to take responsibility for the consequences of his decisions rather than falling back on his pattern of blaming other people.

Another way we can recognize when we are stuck in an old pattern is when our self-defeating mantra is keeping us afraid. Fear is what stops us from speaking up when we have been conditioned to be silent, or what stops us from being authentic instead of hiding behind an uncomfortable joke. We fear letting go of our defenses and we make excuses to keep them. A client once told me that trying out a new response would feel like trying to cross the Grand Canyon in one step. To him, putting his foot over the edge felt like plunging to his death. But in fact, he reported to me, as soon as he did finally pick his foot up, the other bank rushed in, and he landed on solid ground.

We can go after what we need and want by understanding what is keeping us from moving forward and taking responsibility for ourselves and our actions. It isn't easy, but the great thing about the passing years is that we learn how to gain more control of our lives in the present rather than continue to be ruled by our pasts.

Change Can Be Liberating

Change can be difficult, but it can also be liberating: a chance to move away from the "shoulds" we have soaked up, and instead listen to our own feelings and make the adjustments we need. Change is sometimes challenging, but that does not necessarily translate to being undesirable. We need stimulation. We are kept emotionally fit by our ability to respond in new ways as our circumstances, environment, and body change.

When we get away to explore a new place, we feel refreshed by the new sights, smells, and culture. Richer and more exciting environments can enhance our self-esteem. Unfairly, experiments have been done with rats showing that they can withstand the effects of poison better when they are in a stimulating environment as opposed to poor rats stuck in a familiar situation. We can't repeat the experiment with humans, but it goes to show that how we feel emotionally can have physical repercussions too. And this isn't only about going on vacations to foreign lands. We create an internal environment through the people who influence us, through what we read, the stories we imbibe, and how we talk to ourselves. Even when we have no power over our external environment—remember Viktor Frankl?—we usually do have the freedom to use our minds to our advantage or to our detriment.

Many people write to me describing feeling restless and twitchy or dissatisfied, and it can be an indicator that change is afoot or needs to be. It might also be an old pattern of not being able to stick with anything—I'll get to that in a bit. This woman who describes having lost any sense of eagerness or excitement is an example of someone who might benefit from the possibility of change.

> I am thirty-seven, have a lovely husband and a wonderful child, and a job in a creative industry. The problem is that I haven't been happy in my career for a long time and have felt very stuck, and every now and again I end up crying because I just don't know what to do with my life. I was an overachiever in school (worked hard, got good grades, went to an oustanding college) but am now in a role where there is little progression and I'm not sure I even want to stay in this career.
>
> I am realizing that I have spent so much time trying to do what is expected of me that I have absolutely no idea what it is that I want to do. I also cringe at how much I put up with in my twenties. I chased men I knew deep down I didn't really like and took on all kinds of extra tasks at work with the promise that it would look good on my résumé, but got few promotions.
>
> I feel relieved I am at least finally aware of this behavior, but I am terrified that it is too late. I have been applying for jobs, but there are not many firms that want a mother approaching forty. And, like I say, I'm not sure I even want to stay in this field. Please help.

We often receive a strong set of rules from our early life, maybe from our parents or from our culture, that life should be lived in a certain way. Soaking up all these external messages, many of us assume that we should work hard in school, should go to college, should work in a competitive industry, should rise to the top. These may be paths that suit many people, but they by no means suit all. Somehow, something or someone stole the steering wheel of this woman's life, and her job is to get it back.

I think her dissatisfaction comes from her having a sort of board game of years and milestones in mind—of which milestone she should reach by which year. Up until now, as far as work goes, she has been focusing on being seen to be doing the right thing, or doing things for her résumé rather than for her satisfaction in the present. I wonder how many of us are in responsible, professional jobs when we'd rather be, say, working in doggy day care. Perhaps we might be doing work we don't find satisfying, not only for financial reasons, but because we worry what people will think. Ticking the boxes we are expected to tick, grounded in the "shoulds" we have internalized. It is not a helpful game but it's an easy one to fall into.

We get into a habit of being told by others what we want and what we need and what we should do. I've noticed that when someone is very rigid and cannot let anyone new in, or at least not for long, they continue to let in their old beliefs or the people who instilled them in the first place. This makes it difficult, although not impossible, to change tack. What would happen if this woman lessened the impact of her earliest experiences and allowed herself to be more present in the here and now?

If you are feeling restless yet struggling to figure out what it is that you want to change, don't pressure yourself to know. Instead, try this exercise. What comes to your mind when you think about "engagement and excitement"? Think of the word "rewarding" or "fulfillment"—what comes to mind? Write these words down, think about them, and see what comes up for you. Treat this like a sort of meditative brainstorm; don't reject any idea—you might scare away the other ideas. You can't rush this. Jot down images or words that come up when you do this exercise. Then look at those again and see what sticks for you. I think it's a good idea to write down your dreams and see what feelings and images recur in them too. Dreams can furnish us with useful metaphors that can help us work out what we need. It's important to listen to your feelings as you go through this exercise, so you feel motivated to enact the changes that will help you make the most of your life. If you cannot feel, it is impossible to know what you want, and if you don't know what you desire, how can you aim for it?

Everyday Wisdom

In order to know what direction we need to take in life, we need to work out what we're feeling. From understanding our feelings, we can then work out what we want, and when we know what we want, we can go after it.

Sometimes when we are at a crossroad, we freeze as we fear making the wrong choice. It feels like we might avoid mistakes if we don't make decisions. But not making a decision is still a choice and it may, like other choices, be the wrong one. I believe it is impossible to really know whether a choice is the right one without hindsight—and none of us has that. Mistakes and failures are necessary in order to grow. In psychotherapy we sometimes call them "another bloody fucking learning opportunity."

I remember a time in my life when I was very restless. So much so that I had given up my job as a paralegal and leaped into art school. I hoped I'd meet creative types there who would give me the boost I needed, only to find that the legal folk I had left behind were more erudite, thoughtful, and interesting than the art students. I widened my search for something or somebody at evening classes. Signing up for a film appreciation class did not change me. But signing up for a creative writing course had far-reaching consequences.

The course must have been effective because eventually I became a writer, journalist, and broadcaster. This in turn led to my books, including this one. I tend to forget all the other classes I tried that did so much less for me, but I'm very glad I didn't give up trying to find one that suited me just because so many did not. It is too easy to give up too soon. I kept going until I found the class that inspired me, and in doing so I also kept going until I found the partner I wanted to be with too.

It is natural after six attempts at anything, if all six experiences have been bad—maybe job interviews or online dates—to think *I can't do this and this is obviously not for me.* But changing that mindset might be doing ourselves a favor. If one in every fifty cold calls leads to a sale, a trick successful salespeople do is think that the more failed calls they get, the closer they get to a sale—so as time goes on, the more excited they get, the more enthusiasm they display, making it more likely that they'll succeed. And as any salesperson of the year will tell you, they do succeed. Be less pessimistic: be more salesperson.

You never know how things are going to turn out. My advice is to try enough things and then hopefully life becomes one big, exciting adventure of discovery. The great thing is you can always start a new business or retrain for a different job or profession, and, if you can afford it, take a break to try out other things to see if you like them. A friend of mine co-founded a new creative industry business at eighty, so I don't think you've lost if you haven't got to a certain age without a particular milestone. We don't need to play that game. Get off those paths and find another game.

> ## Everyday Wisdom
>
> Be less pessimistic about trying new things. Even if what you try doesn't work out, you will be one step closer to where you want to be.

I think the biggest risk you can take is staying in a place that's making you unhappy or that makes you feel stale. However, if you do change your job, your partner, your home every two weeks, then your new experience would be to find out what you could learn if you tried something and stuck with it. One size does not fit all, but one size that often fits is to answer the questions "What are my fears?," and "How are my fears holding me back?" What might happen if you felt the fear and did it anyway? Embrace moments of change not as a frightening unknown but as an opportunity to uncover and pursue your desires. At first it will feel like letting go of a rope and not knowing where the ground is. It can be scary. But more often than not, solid ground is only two inches below your feet.

How to Change Old Habits

Sometimes, one of my psychotherapy clients will be late. "The subway got stuck—I do apologize." If it happens once, I don't treat it as significant. But some clients are perpetually late and out of breath when they get to the door—perhaps just five or ten minutes, but every time. Then I am curious about what is behind their pattern of lateness, what it means, and what purpose it serves.

There are probably as many reasons for unpunctuality as there are habitually late people. One client remembered that his mother always spent so long in the bathroom that she made him late for school. She told him it didn't matter, and early people are uptight anyway. In his unconscious, being on time for things had got mixed up with being disloyal to his mother and was therefore bad. Once he had found this narrative, he lost his compulsion for lateness. Or perhaps they are unreasonably optimistic about how many things they can cram in and how long it takes to get from the office to the restaurant, say, especially if it's nearby. My book editor and I often have lunch in a café next door to her office and she is always seven minutes late because she leaves at 1 p.m. I think she believes she possesses a teleporter, but by the time she has chatted to a colleague in the lobby and waited for the elevator, she is seven minutes late.

Some late people choose to accept that they are terrible timekeepers and that they can't do anything about it. We often talk to ourselves in a defeatist way by saying "This is just the way I am," or "I can't change that," but we can clock such excuses and decide to experiment despite them. We don't just reach adulthood and stop developing. The brain is plastic; we can therefore change it. We change it by noticing what we normally do, inhibit our normal reaction, and work to form an alternative response, and thus develop a new habit.

Think of your brain as if it had a highway running through it. That highway is your old way of responding to a situation. On the other hand, a new habit or behavior is like hacking an uncharted path through the jungle with a machete. The old way is easy and automatic—you put yourself on autopilot and go. But the new way is hard work: You need to think about where you're going and what you're doing, and it requires effort and strength. To return to the punctuality example, it is only when the latecomers make the decision to be punctual that they change. It must be a conscious decision; if they merely make a half-hearted attempt to "try" to be on time, they won't be. Their brain will revert to the highway, and they will continue to be late.

Beware when you're under stress or pressure not to jump back on the highway as it's normal to return to the easy and familiar route when our energy is occupied elsewhere. I think parents find this happens to them. Perhaps they are adamant that they will never behave in the way that their parents behaved, but when they're under stress, they find themselves reverting to the ways in which they were raised.

As another example of someone wanting to change a particular habit, let's look at this letter from a woman who is finding it hard to stop gossiping at work.

> I can't seem to stop gossiping and complaining about the people around me. This primarily happens at work, and I am not the only person who does it; it is a toxic environment where bitching is the norm, so it is hard to resist. Every day I give myself a little talk about how I am not going to say a bad word about someone and every day I get sucked into gossip or end up saying something mean. It is the trait I deplore the most in

myself and I am starting to believe that deep down I am a horrible person who doesn't deserve any friends. I used to pride myself on my ability to be honest, opinionated, and outspoken, but the balance has tipped into bitterness, whining, and impulsive gossiping. The worst part is, when I bitch about someone, I deep down don't feel negatively about them and am baffled as to why I say such horrible things.

I have worked hard on myself in the last few years (becoming sober, going to therapy) and I am ashamed that I have not evolved into a better person. I don't want to be small-minded by getting a thrill out of bringing others down. I really respect and admire people who are more positive, open-minded, and can control their thoughts and emotions around others—how do I become that person and say goodbye once and for all to this poisonous part of myself?

By recognizing and articulating her problem, this woman is already well on the way to changing tack. It is difficult to stop gossiping, especially if we feel insecure in our environment. It is an expedient way to bond with someone when there is a third party that you both agree is in some way bad. As the socialite and wit Alice Roosevelt Longworth once said: "If you've got nothing nice to say . . . come and sit by me." Gossip can work as a glue: It flows between people who feel mutually friendly and it's a sign that there is trust between them. It can relieve feelings of tension or animosity we may have toward people as it can release pressure we may have felt. Yet there are downsides too. If we hear negative gossip about someone, it can change the way we think about them, which can be unfair and harsh. Neither is it great when it's our turn to be the subject of the gossip. Of course, if we find a tactful way of more direct communication that may be better for everyone.

When we experiment with something new, it's normal to be of two minds about it. Sometimes it feels the amount of good something is going to do us is in direct proportion to how much dread we feel when contemplating it: think running a marathon when you've only ever run to catch the bus, or quitting drinking completely after spending the pandemic with a wine glass as your companion. It's odd how difficult embracing improving changes can be. A hit of dopamine reinforces a bad habit, and we'll tell ourselves any old baloney to get another hit. That's what this woman might be experiencing in her attempt to quit gossiping.

But changes that make a positive difference don't have to be dramatic; they can be tiny, fine-tuned adjustments, such as deciding to cultivate a different variety of plant or learning a new word a day. I would suggest to this woman that she try to get into the habit of "I" statements. So instead of "he is irritating" switch to noticing "I feel irritated," thus taking responsibility for her reactions and realizing that just because someone irritates us it doesn't mean there is anything wrong with them. This habit will help her take responsibility for her response rather than blaming the other. It might not be as fun as moaning to our best office friend, but it could be more useful. Even when we make a very small difference to our routine or outlook, it can make a significant impact on our feelings of well-being.

I also observe that she is very hard on herself for gossiping. She can already articulate her problem and she is at the stage of catching herself after she's done it, so she is on the right track. I am reminded of Portia Nelson's poem, "An Autobiography in Five Chapters." It's about walking down a road and falling down a hole. She falls in, and it's not her fault. Then she sees the hole, she knows she's going to fall in, she does fall in, and it's still not her fault. After which she sees the hole, she falls in, and it is her fault. She sees the hole, and she walks around it. Then she walks down another street entirely. Her metaphor means that we need to cut ourselves some slack when we are learning a new habit: It takes time to change behavior. So instead of beating ourselves up when we are tempted to fall into bad habits, we can congratulate ourselves for our awareness—"Aha! That's what I don't want to do anymore!" Defer judging altogether and be curious about yourself. Notice your progress, notice the temptations, and high-five yourself when you don't act on them.

If you are ready to shift an old habit or try something new, here's my recommendation: Get a large piece of plain paper and draw a circle in the middle. Inside the circle, write examples of activities that you feel completely comfortable doing. In mine, I might put something like going for a short walk. Around the outside of that circle, write down examples of activities that you can do but that you have to push yourself a little bit to do. For example, climbing to the top of a monument or hill. Draw a larger circle around this circle of activities. In the next band, write activities that you would like to do but feel some trepidation about. These might be things like a seven-day walk, approaching someone with a new business idea, or starting a charity. Draw another circle around this ring of activities. Write down those things you are far too scared to try but harbor ambitions about—maybe putting yourself forward for public office. Create as many circles as you like.

In time, the activities immediately outside our inner circle become commonplace and our comfort zone expands. What may be in an outer circle might well be in someone else's inner circle, but we should remember that whatever we try is for ourselves alone. It doesn't matter what anyone else might think. Experiment with new things and if the experiment doesn't make you feel more stimulated, more interconnected, more alive, no harm will have been done and you can drop it. The idea is to expand in small steps. In my experience, I have found that if we don't test our limits from time to time, our comfort zone can shrink.

The main thing to remember is that change takes practice. It might not feel right at the start because it won't feel familiar, and we mistake familiarity for truth. What is familiar and comfortable feels right, even if it harms us.

So keep on walking and hacking away at the jungle and tread on those new paths. The more you tread on them, the more natural they will feel until they become as automatic as a highway.

With Change Comes Loss

Sometimes we are the agents of change and those changes are desirable, but at other times change is thrust upon us when we didn't necessarily want it. How can we cope with that? It's important to acknowledge that with change often comes loss, especially when we were not ready for things to change. When a relationship shifts— from lovers to companions, friends to acquaintances, carer to cared-for—there will be losses to mourn, whether that's for an old way of life or for how a relationship used to be and how you used to be within that relationship.

Even if you expect and accept the change, it can still create a void within you that your psyche will try to fill. A common example is a parent experiencing their child separating from them for the first time. It can feel hurtful to parents when teenagers rebel or reject them or politely refuse to join in or turn down their suggestions or loving advice. It is less hurtful if the parent can manage to see it as a part of the teenager becoming themselves.

That's also why a breakup can feel like a bereavement: You are experiencing loss. You will miss them, and you will miss who you were when you were with them. You will be worrying about how you will manage and you will resent having to worry about that, because had this breakup not happened, you wouldn't have had to apply yourself to these new circumstances. You may feel trepidation: You are leaving the familiar and stepping into the unknown. You might have more philosophical worries too: Who are you now in your new single state? How has it changed your individual identity? I think about these questions with regard to a letter I received from a woman in her midthirties, whose relationship fell apart while simultaneously going through fertility treatment.

> I was in a relationship for ten years with someone I love very deeply and thought I'd grow old with. We recently started to have medically assisted IUI (intrauterine insemination) with donor sperm (we're lesbians) and then my partner left me two days before our first try. I found out she'd been having an affair with a mutual friend. She came back for a while, and we had a lot of love and intimacy, yet she then left again.
>
> I'd been going to our clinic for three weeks, and I feel so sad and as though I can't let go of what I thought was going to be our baby. It also doesn't feel as if there's any language for this as fertility treatment for lesbians is not really in society "speak," so I'm struggling to even name what's happened to me. I also understand that affairs are symptomatic of wider problems, and I want to own my part in the breakdown—our

communication had entirely broken down as my partner now says she really didn't want our baby.

I realize now that my partner had been slowly withdrawing over the two years of planning (we chose names, schools, places to live, saved money, talked about how and when we'd have our second child), and when I tried to talk to her, she stonewalled me so much that in the end I just got angry and needed some sort of connection, even if it was a negative one.

How the hell do I process and accept all of this, and how am I meant to move on and be OK? I can't get beyond feeling as though I am a failure and have hugely malfunctioned, which isn't rational, I know, but I feel so floored. I'm also not sure if I ought to pursue motherhood solo. Would I be enough for my child? It feels very punishing. And so lonely.

When a person leaves us, it can feel that we also lose the part of us we were when we were together and the future we had envisioned for ourselves with that person. That gap in us can feel like a raw wound. Of course this woman is devastated. She lost her partner and the dream of parenting with her. The other person that left her is that baby she dreamed of, and the person that baby would have developed into. Whether the dream is a child, a new house, a new relationship, a new country, there is a period of mourning to be got through when it doesn't materialize. If we have a vision and it is nearly within our grasp, and then snatched away, a lot of the feelings we have are likely to be similar to when we lose a person who was important to us. And just like mourning the death of a loved one, there's no speeding that process up, but in time the wound will heal, or we get used to it, or grow around it so it becomes more background for us.

I get many letters sent to me about getting through a breakup or any other unexpected and undesired life changes, and my biggest piece of advice is to open the tap and let the feelings out, otherwise the pressure will build up. It can become like an obsession, coloring every aspect of your life. If you feel stuck in the obsessional stage, you can move beyond it by controlling where and when you let it out. You do this by setting a timetable for it. Weep, rage, and mourn at the same time every day for half an hour. In fact, you must mourn and grieve then, even if you don't feel like it. Reminisce about the way life used to be. You could make a shrine, light a candle, weep, write a love letter that you will never send—anything— but no more than half an hour a day and only at your allotted time. Be strict, set alarms. In this way while you are having your feelings and working through them, you are also gaining control of them. It will take determination and will- power, but like any skill, you will improve with

Everyday Wisdom

It sounds bizarre, setting a timer to obsess, but it teaches us to get control over our thoughts rather than our thoughts having control over us.

practice. And maybe in some of your grieving half hours, you can get a friend or family member to hold you while you weep. You don't have to do this on your own. But don't forget to set the timer.

I would give that same advice to this young woman who is planning to have surgery to reduce her risk of breast cancer.

I am a twenty-six-year-old woman, and I tested positive for the BRCA gene mutation five years ago. This means that, over the course of my lifetime, I have a very high chance of developing breast cancer because (without getting too technical) my body doesn't have the ability to recognize certain cancerous cells and fight against them.

I knew at the time of getting my results that I would want to have a risk-reducing mastectomy and I am now at a stage in my life (in my career and relationships) where I feel ready to do it. Even though the doctors have told me that my life expectancy is the same whether or not I have the surgery—if I don't have it, I am very likely to develop cancer, but as I will start regular screening, they're also very likely to catch it—I know that the surgery is the right option for me. The thought of going for screenings every year, knowing one day they will come back positive, is not something I want for myself. I'd rather have the surgery now and live peacefully.

My mom had breast cancer and passed away after being in treatment for years, and she was with me when

I received the results of my BRCA test (she was also positive). I remember her feeling very guilty and upset for me, but I was fine. Once upon a time that may have been a death sentence, but now there are so many options for me, and I feel very lucky to have the diagnosis because I have options that my mom never had. I saw this as just another thing that I would have to do now that I am an adult, and as long as I could plan for it, then it would be OK. My breasts are small and not a big part of my self-image, so I never thought I would miss them that much.

But now that I am getting closer to my surgery, I feel panicked and overwhelmed a lot of the time. I find it difficult to focus on anything else, but I don't want to annoy my friends and family by constantly talking about it. I know the surgery is something that I want, and I also know that now is the right time for it, so why do I feel this way?

We think about mourning when we lose someone close to us: when we lose a parent, partner, pet, or friend, everyone around us expects us to be sad or angry or confused, in denial, or simply deadened for a while—wherever the journey of mourning takes us. Even if it is a hard journey, we know that unless we allow ourselves to mourn, we won't recover our equilibrium. The only way beyond loss is through it.

It's much harder to understand when the loss we experience is something other than another soul we were bonded to. Often nobody notices or names it, and there is no expectation that we may have grief work to do. What this young woman is experiencing after the loss of her mother is another loss: the loss of her breasts, which are a part of her femininity, and of her body being whole and unscarred.

She feels grateful that she can have the risk of developing cancer significantly reduced by having an operation, but you can be grateful and sad and panicked at the same time. Why wouldn't you panic if the area of your body that is under so much medical scrutiny is the same part that killed your mother? Why wouldn't you be anxious if currently healthy tissue is going to be surgically removed from you in an operation?

Difficult feelings are hard enough to talk about, but if we censure ourselves for having those feelings, that's when they become impossible to manage. Instead of finding loving support for the process of grieving, we might lock ourselves in a silent, agonizing world in which we feel increasingly isolated. When the task of processing loss doesn't happen in us, it can take over our entire world and cloud everything else. We might feel that if we own the disappointment and

> **Everyday Wisdom**
>
> Part of the process of change is to accept that there will be a part of us that needs to mourn. You can be grateful for the change while also grieving the way things were.

name the gaps, our feelings will become more intense and unmanageable, but the opposite is true. To talk about loss is to begin to process those feelings and is the first step to healing.

The thing that we think makes us the most unusual, isolated, or lonely is often the thing that makes us feel the most connected when we share it with others. I think this may be because, if we manage to put into words feelings that are not often articulated and sincerely describe how we feel, two things happen. One: By articulating the feeling we make sense of it, we understand it more, and we understand ourselves more. And two: If we can manage to communicate that to another person, then our words might help them to understand some of their feelings too. When we share how we really think and feel, how we really are, and someone can understand us, that is where connection happens. Such connection is healing. We are allowed to be vulnerable and sad, to grieve, to feel loss, and to give ourselves time to get over the shock and to adapt to a different body.

Accepting Aging

The idea of there being such things as children and adults is but a construct of our own making. We don't just magically switch into being a grown-up at twenty-one or whenever being an adult is supposed to start. I spent my late teens and twenties waiting for some miraculous switch to happen when I no longer felt like myself, which I knew was being a child, and became something much more sensible, which is called an adult.

So that sudden switch to adulthood doesn't happen, but over time we do change. Life does impact us, changing us and possibly even developing us into someone more evolved today than we were yesterday. What tends to change, though, is our content, not our processes. Let me explain: "Content" is the story and "process" is the pattern of the actions. So for example, if we are a worrier, what we worry about—the story—will change, but the fact that we are always worrying does not. A small child might be worrying about the leaves dying and falling off a tree. When they grow up, they might no longer care about the leaves, but they will experience the same feelings of worry about another story—like worrying about who to send a Christmas card to. Our evolution into older people does not mean that we change into completely different people, and it is important to remember that. For me, the main change is that I feel exhausted more of the time.

Growing older is something we all must contend with, yet it can be a difficult process to accept and navigate. Physically our body changes and that isn't easy. Aging can mean the loss of mobility, needing to rest more, and not being able to do what you may have previously taken for granted. However philosophical you are about these changes, if you think about them, they involve loss too.

You are allowed to mourn for the way things were, to acknowledge the effect that change can have on you. It is natural to long for a time in your life when you were younger and more vital.

We are trained from an early age to believe youth is beauty and age is not, particularly if you are a woman. I remember my mother looking at herself and bemoaning her loss of youth and saying stuff to me like "It's all right for you…" But it wasn't all right for me because she was passing down the habit of body hatred and shame. We are bombarded with images of very young women together with messages that this is what we should all look like. You'd think because of this stereotype that these young girls are the epitome of womanhood, but they are not.

An example of someone struggling with accepting her aging body is a woman who wrote to me asking for advice on how to feel more confident in her skin.

How can I be less self-conscious and full of self-hatred about my untoned, middle-aged, sagging body when unclothed? This means I'm inhibited in many ways and avoid activities where I need to show my arms, and even worse, my legs, or my belly. I dread having to wear a swimsuit, even though I do enjoy swimming. It also means I don't feel comfortable being naked with my partner during sex. It even affects which positions we take; I can't bring myself to be on top as I feel so ashamed of my sagging belly and breasts.

I walk a lot, go to yoga, Pilates, and other classes several times a week, and love what my body can achieve in these classes. I'm almost sixty and have a good diet (plenty of fish, legumes, fruit, and a wide range of vegetables). I am overweight by twenty pounds and have struggled with this most of my life. Maybe this is relevant—at an early age I developed large breasts that attracted unwanted male attention when I was still essentially a child, and I remember choosing clothes to disguise my womanly body rather than celebrate it.

I know that we are all much more than our physical appearance and I feel ashamed of being ashamed. I don't look at my friends with disgust; they're gorgeous, despite not having perfect bodies, so why do I look at myself that way?

Our skin sags as it ages, and we have been conditioned to think of it as not beautiful. We've been told what we are supposed to look like by people trying to sell us firming lotions and antiaging creams and fashions. Their goal is to fill us with fear that we will be unlovable due to not looking like a twenty-year-old and they feed our self-disgust so we buy more stuff, and it works. Well, in so far as their tactics work to make us buy the stuff; the stuff, no, that doesn't work, and our skin and fat distribution remain appropriate to our age.

We can look at skin that looks like crêpe paper where there was once smooth flesh, and we can know we have been trained to believe one is good and the other bad. We can also know we have a choice about how we think about this. Who are the most attractive older women really? Not the slimmest, not the ones who look the youngest, but the women who carry themselves with pride, who don't hide away, who hold their heads up and laugh, never mind what might wobble; the ones who are breathing because they aren't holding their breath as they try to suck in a stomach. Confidence is attractive. We must try to develop it. Confidence, not thinness or firmness, is the key to feeling beautiful.

This is generalized and of course men are subject to aging too, and gay men in particular are subject to the critical gaze of others. But there is an added pressure on women to look young because we have always been culturally subjected to the male gaze—the women's mags telling us to look a certain way, the wolf whistling, the catcalling, the ass grabbing at bus stops and in clubs—and for many of us the male gaze has become our own gaze.

The woman who wrote to me questioned whether it was relevant that she received unwanted male attention as a child, and I think it's hugely relevant. That attention made her feel horrible, and she thought it was her body making her feel horrible because she felt invaded, scared, and repulsed when having inappropriate sexualized remarks aimed at her. Her unconscious made sense of these comments by thinking *If I didn't have my body, I wouldn't feel disgusted and scared.* Unwanted attention makes us far more conscious of our physical appearance, so when our body changes with age, we can find it disorientating. I know some men also feel a lack of confidence in their body, but I do believe that generally men are better at patting their potbellies and smiling. The level of anxiety that women feel about their bodies changing tends to be different.

As I have said before, it is easy to mistake familiarity for truth. Who is to declare what is beautiful and what is not? If you relate to the woman who wrote the letter, I want you to hold your head up proudly. You have a wonderful, sexy body. Practice being proud of it. Don't waste another day of not relishing just how fabulous you are. You may not feel confident, but act it, get used to it. You can fake it to make it.

Another letter that I think well describes the experience of aging is one by a retired woman who felt like she had been left behind by the technological advances of the modern world.

> As a retired woman living alone, I felt isolated during the various lockdowns. The answer seemed to be to rely on technology, which was fine when it worked, but it often made me feel more cut off from the world. For example, when I didn't know how to unmute myself on a video call it was like having locked-in syndrome. Emerging from the pandemic, things are better, except COVID-19 has made technology the way forward and I can't always get it to work for me.

I've been to a restaurant where I had to forgo lunch because I couldn't order on the app. I have a smartphone I often struggle with—for months I didn't know how to answer a call, so I had to wait for people to leave a voice mail, then I had to call them back.

If I buy a new device, it doesn't even come with a manual to show me how it works. I am drifting further apart from people who use their phones and watches (watches?!) for everything. I don't feel I belong in this world. And this is unlikely to get better.

A confession first: I also find it a pain in the neck how we must increasingly rely on technology. I can't even work my own central heating system and I can't pay my domestic property tax without having to remember a password. When the internet first arrived, I was quite good, but nothing ever stays still; the word "update" makes me shudder. As you get the hang of one video-conferencing app, it updates, or it's replaced with a different program entirely and then you must relearn how to use it. I've become bored of watching YouTube videos trying to educate myself. Younger people can fiddle and adapt to technology intuitively: They've grown up with it. We haven't. Rant aside, learning something new is good for our older brains. We can learn more than we often give ourselves credit for. Go to technology stores and ask for help. I find I must ask for help more than once because I need to be told it a few times and practice it before it sticks.

The great thing about being old is that we can say exactly how we feel and what we want and usually get away with it. One thing you can clap us oldies for, if you like, is learning not to care so much about what other people think of us. (Note I said "so much." We veer toward the psychopathic if we don't care at all about others.)

I asked my grandmother, when she was a hundred, what the advantage was to being that age, and she said: "Now, at last, I can say exactly what I like and get away with it." Cheers for that, Gran.

But there is something else going on here. Most people feel they're not at the center of a group, and more at the edges. There is a part of this woman (and you, reader, and me, and all of us) destined to remain alone, unseen. So, if growing older makes you feel like you are left behind and destined to aloneness, I want you to know that you are not alone: There is an unseen, unknown part to all of us. You do belong in this world, even if a part of you may sometimes feel that you don't.

Coping with Grief

The death of someone we love is a moment of profound change in our lives. The letters I receive about grief are among the most touching and profound. I sometimes say that the price of love is grief, and in many of these letters, you can feel the depth and weight of the love they continue to carry. This letter from a grieving mother is one of many that have stayed with me.

> I am a mom of three, but one of my children died as a baby. The other two are now thirty-four and twenty-nine, and because I think I have been subconsciously trying to keep them alive ever since, I have become their go-to support, emotionally (relationships, work, lack of, friendships—anything really), financially, and physically (I will drop everything to be by their side whenever necessary).
>
> This also impacts my husband, who provides the finances, and though he is extremely generous, he cannot understand the bond I have with them and why they turn to me so much (he doesn't have children of his own and would not have dreamed of calling his own parents in such circumstances as my children call me). The problem lies with me, obviously. I worry day and night, suffer night terrors regularly as well as insomnia, and I have an overwhelming feeling of failure as a parent coupled with pressure to make them happy somehow—I took antidepressants even before my twins were born because I had a difficult childhood and lost both parents at a very young age, but was determined to overcome depression without drugs because of the side effects, but now I feel pretty much broken. How can I change and deal with this?

I feel so much for that young girl who lost her parents, and that vulnerable young part of her seems to exist within her still. I expect any sort of normal sense of security was stolen from her then. After that, it's only normal to fear that bad things might happen to the significant people in her life. And even if she had started to recover, losing a baby would have reopened the old wound of losing her parents. Her fears are understandable.

When old trauma lies buried deep within our bones, it doesn't show itself in so many words but is more of a free-floating anxiety or an inchoate persistent worry— and we can't just bat this away with logic. It is not a sign that we are broken. Only a sign that we have been made more sensitive to the fragility of life. When we have suffered a great loss, we cannot easily take it for granted that the people around us won't leave us too, and a happy-go-lucky, go-with-the-flow approach to life is often replaced with a less flexible, more fearful way of being in the world. One of the problems with this is that when everything is going right, rather than enjoy it, we can be scared it will be taken away. I encourage people who are struggling with this, like the woman who wrote this letter, to try to live more in the present rather than the past or future. We can do this, especially when going to sleep, by replacing worrying thoughts and focusing on the sounds and sensations of our breath.

Sometimes we grow around the grief, but it's there as big as it ever was. Sometimes it seems to come in waves and feels as acute as it first did. There are theories, such as stages of grief that you pass through and then come out the other side. In my experience of life and death, very few people can relate to this sort of theory. Bereavement goes on its own journey and people experience it in their own ways. This letter from a woman who continues to grieve her mother decades after her death is a reminder that we do not grieve to a set plan.

> I am fifty years old, live a privileged life with my husband and our two children, and really don't want for much. My mother died very suddenly when I was twenty-five—she was sixty-one. Her death was from a heart attack. We had no clue that she was gravely ill. My father died of bowel cancer at age eighty-one.
>
> While it was very sad to see my dad's decline, I felt able to come to terms with his illness and subsequent death. However—and the reason I'm seeking guidance—I don't think I ever really learned how to deal with my mom's death. Even now, tears are coming to my eyes as I write this. How can this be right after twenty-five years? I should be over it.
>
> I briefly saw a counselor, who suggested I immerse myself in my mom—listen to her favorite songs, etc. This did not help. I still feel like I haven't dealt with her death. I'd be grateful for any insights as to how to deal with this.

What is clear to me is that this woman lost her mother too young, it was a terrible shock, and at a time in her life when she was still developing in relationship with her.

Some people can and do fill the gap inside themselves that a significant person dying has left, but it is hard to do this when you haven't finished getting to know them, and I think this is especially so with a parent who dies too soon.

There's a school of therapy founded by Fritz and Laura Perls called Gestalt. A commonly used Gestalt intervention is to put two chairs out. One for you and one that remains empty for the person with whom you have unfinished business. And, daft as it sounds, you tell the chair that represents the missing person everything you need to say to them, out loud. Then—and this is the clever bit—you sit in their empty chair and be them, and respond to your empty chair with what you imagine they would say back to you. If you are grieving, this exercise might help you cathartically release your tears, which you probably need to do, and might help you if you feel stuck in your grief.

Everyday Wisdom

Think about grief not as something to "deal" with but as something to "feel" with instead. Try not to resent your grief or push it away, but to make friends with the pain and the sadness.

Like this woman, many of us might want our grief "dealt with." If you relate to her frustration, I want you to switch the "deal with" to "feel with." Feelings, I'm afraid, will not be dealt with. It's not how they work. You cannot scold a child out of a tantrum, nor yourself from feeling grief. Parts of ourselves don't die just because we move on, they remain dormant until something reignites them. Old men on their deathbeds call for their mothers and you cannot help but feel deeply for them. I encourage anyone grieving not to resent their grief or to want to rid themselves of it. It might sound weird, because at times grief is as agonizing and raw as it ever was, and here I am saying don't push it away. But if we can experiment with not being embarrassed or angry when the tears come, and instead accept that they will and they are part of how we love, they may become easier to live with.

Benjamin Franklin said there were only two things certain in life: death and taxes. We cannot bring our loved ones back. What we can do is change our relationship with grief. When we push grief away, it'll come back harder. When we welcome it, look after it, feel kindly toward it, cease being afraid of it, it will not go away, but it will be easier to carry. We hurt because we lost someone we love and we will always have deep emotions about this, but we can make friends with the sadness and not necessarily feel it less but mind it less.

In my book *How to Stay Sane*, I talk about sanity as the path between being too rigid or too chaotic. That path is about being flexible—being able to accept change, bring about change where necessary, and even embrace it. To be human is to want to belong, and to feel we have a role and a place in society. Probably the most important changes we bring about are those to improve our sense of belonging—being part of a family, choosing our work environment, or even joining an online group. Belonging is an important foundation for contentment, which we will tackle in the next chapter.

4.   How We Find Contentment

Discovering Inner Peace, Fulfillment, and Meaning

One of the things that I find often gets in the way of our contentment is how much importance we collectively place on being happy. Happiness is feeling pleasure: It is a heightened state. Think of it as a spike of delighted surprise when you get a text from a friend you are pleased to hear from, or when you can finish work early and have time to walk in the sun. I look at happiness as a short-term feeling. It would be impossible to be happy all the time.

Instead, I'd like this final chapter to focus on what contentment looks like for you. Contentment is about being satisfied with your life; it is a default background state that we can aim for in the long term. If we can accept all our emotions—the difficult ones as well as the pleasurable ones—we can use them to guide us in our lives. This chapter aims to help you understand and manage all these different emotions, in order to help you develop your capacity for happiness and build a base of background contentment.

Managing Stress and Anxiety

There are stressful aspects to every age: passing exams, getting a job you want, sticking at a job you hate, conflict, wanting a partner, drought, wanting children, the trap of baby jail, financial worries, housing worries, loneliness, divorce, relevance, meaning, striving for bigger accomplishments, more money, later babies, stronger bodies, better sex, smoother skin, learning when you have to slow down, planning for the last years of your life, dealing with increasing infirmity. It is stressful doing something that stretches you, something that you have not done before and that might not work. Or, worse, you achieved what you had set out to do, but you don't feel the relief you had imagined it would bring. At any age we can be faced with the challenge of having to reconcile our inner picture of ourselves to our external reality.

We experience stress and anxiety for myriad reasons, and it can be momentary or long-lasting. But not all stress is bad: Stressing yourself is a way of keeping your brain fit. No stress at all means you are not getting a mental workout. Good stress creates positive stimulation, pushing us to learn new things and to be creative, without being so overwhelming that it tips us into panic. Learning things causes us to form new neural connections, and the more of these we have, the better. If a part of your brain were to die off, having more neural connections means that other parts of your brain can link up more quickly to go around the damaged part.

You can, though, have too much of a good thing. Ongoing, continuous high levels of stress lead to panic and dissociation. Dissociation is a disconnect between our thoughts, sensations, feelings, and actions, and is experienced as a sort of blanking out. Panic and dissocia-tion can lead to burnout, so what can you do to avoid them?

I received a letter from a young man who struggled with stress and anxiety to the extent that it was getting in the way of his everyday life.

> I am a thirty-two-year-old man with a successful career and a loving girlfriend. I've suffered my fair share of trauma in my childhood and adult life and have some health issues. The problem I have right now is that my anxiety levels are so high that every morning I am fro-zen in fear. I struggle to get washed and dressed and have no motivation to get up and go.
>
> But it isn't really just that. I feel physically sick at the thought of leaving the safe confines of my bedroom. I tend to watch the same TV shows for escapism over and over again. The only time I truly feel safe is at night when everyone is asleep and I'm alone—the world is quiet and it's just me.
>
> I fear disaster and fear people expecting things of me. I am scared I will be trapped in their expectations, and I won't be able to meet them. I'm so demotivated at work and struggle to actually perform as I should. I have a high-pressure job and feel deeply insecure all the time. What can I do?

Alone time is a way for this man to regain equilibrium. Replaying a TV program in which he knows exactly what is going to happen means he has control of the future because he can predict with accuracy the outcome. It's understandable that he finds this soothing as he has had trauma in his life. We will explore trauma more deeply later in this chapter, but often it means having shocks. It sounds as if this man keeps his body in a constant state of readiness. His tense muscles are eager to prepare him so that he won't be shocked next time "it" happens—whatever "it" is. Like him, we can fall into the trap of organizing our bodies in relationship to our past and not to our present. We can get attached to worry in this way and it isn't as helpful as we unconsciously assume.

To manage stress, we develop certain coping mechanisms. Some may use talking things over openly; others use meditation, psychotherapy, religion, or exercise. Other coping strategies are not as helpful: alcoholism, overworking, being obsessed with how things look at the expense of how they feel. To pull an all-nighter, to obsess about work, neglect your bodily needs, have no personal or social life is fine as an emergency stopgap, so long as that emergency mode does not become the norm. The less healthy ways of coping sometimes become unsustainable and trigger a crisis when the body cracks or rebels about how it is being used. A woman wrote to me because an old eating disorder resurfaced, decades after she believed she had recovered, because of the pandemic and the death of her husband. Anorexia was an old coping mechanism and it's no wonder she went back to it in a moment of intense stress. And she's not alone: Many of us fell back into self-destructive behavior during the pandemic because it was a stressful and overwhelming time. There is no shame in having moments when there is too much to cope with. Our strength is not in our resilience, it is in recognizing and owning our vulnerability. The last thing someone in a difficult position needs is to feel ashamed—we need help and compassion, starting with our own self-compassion.

If you need to stop your thoughts racing, I'll remind you again to notice your breathing. Try it now: Stop reading this for ten seconds or so and notice how you breathe. Take twenty seconds now, and it doesn't matter if it's longer or shorter than that—I really want you to notice your in-breath and then your out-breath. This is you having contact with yourself in the present. When you notice how you are breathing, do you slow your breathing down? Before you get up in the morning, lie in bed and be aware of your breath for a minute or two. Your attention will wander; bring it back to your breath. I don't know about you, but I paused typing for a moment and did this exercise and I felt the tiniest bit calmer—each bit of calming helps. Five minutes a day concentrating on your breath can make a positive difference.

Similarly, if you are feeling anxious, a useful exercise to practice is to scan your body to notice which of your muscles are tight and which are loose. I like to use the example of a rescue dog. Imagine you take in a rescue dog. You put your hand up to stroke it, and it flinches in response because it is afraid you might hit it. This reaction is based on past experiences, but it has become an instinctual way for the dog to organize its body in the present. We are the same way. If we were hypervigilant in our past for whatever reason, our body remains tense in the present and this in turn affects how we feel. We hold emotion in our body. What we can do is notice how we organize our body when we are thinking or feeling certain things, and then we can start to undo that. Experiment tightening where you are already tight and collapsing where you are loose, one notch at a time, and notice how you feel as you do this. Does it make you feel more or less anxious? Does it soothe or stress you? It's easier to tense up more than it is to just relax, and when we become more aware of how we make ourselves tense, we can begin to learn how to disorganize that system. This exercise will also help you get out of your mind and into your senses.

Another technique I recommend to stop anxiety whirling around in your head is to put your fears down on paper in a numbered list. Make it as specific as you can. Then change all the what-ifs into so-whats and notice how altering your language makes you feel. I believe everyone needs to develop and maintain their inner observer. Noticing what you're feeling when you're stressed, anxious, or super busy may not be your top priority, but it does need to be up there because our feelings are like lights on a car dashboard. We wouldn't think that taking out a car's fuel-warning bulb was the best driving strategy, and in the same way, we need to observe our feelings rather than repress them. They are there to tell us when we need to rest, to play, to connect with others. When we ignore feelings, they shout louder; in other words, make us feel worse. To ignore feelings and not take them into account means risking a mutiny of emotion. Feelings are like employees: Ignore them or repress them and they will rebel. My advice is to listen to them, take their reports into account when making your decisions, and harness them to help. We want neither to ignore nor to be ruled by them. As with most things, we want a middle ground, which means making our decisions by consulting both head and heart.

When we observe our emotions, we can use them rather than be used *by* them. This means noticing a feeling when it begins to emerge, listening to it, and only then taking action. When we observe a feeling, we run less chance of becoming that feeling. Going back to the man who wrote to me, there is a difference between saying "I am scared" and "I

> ### Everyday Wisdom
>
> Observe your feelings but don't become them. This means keeping a tiny bit of you neutral to do the observing rather than allowing your feelings to overwhelm you completely.

feel scared." "I am scared" is defining a whole person, whereas with "I feel scared" there is a part of the person that is sitting back and observing, and therefore still available to make a decision. We can take our feelings into account without being merely a reaction to those feelings.

So how can we develop our observer part? I recommend keeping a journal of moods, sensations, and observations. This is a part of you that simply observes the different emotions and sensations you have—not part of your gratitude, or your anxiety, or your love, or your fear. Speak from this part. This means instead of saying "I'm anxious," you'll say "I notice I am feeling anxious." Create a sense of distance between you and your negative feeling. You can even separate further by giving it a persona, calling it "Mr./Ms. Anxiety" or whatever seems right. It's a small tweak but you'll find that it makes a difference. When I gave this advice to the man who wrote to me, he responded and told me that labeling his anxiety and giving it a name had made more of a difference than he would have thought possible. It is also likely that sharing how he felt, even in an email to a stranger, lessened his burden as writing it all down gave him a chance to observe himself rather than be fully consumed by his anxiety.

Many people write to me specifically about stress and overwhelm at work. We all know there are statistics about burnout, but what we can do to look after ourselves as an individual can only go so far—the culture is culpable too. If we contribute to a culture where it is only OK to show strength but not vulnerability, we are part of the problem. If we value profits above the people who create them, we are part of the problem. I believe that the immorality of getting as much as we can from employees and contractors for as little as we can get away with should not be hidden behind offers of counseling sessions and mindfulness workshops. Disregarding our workers is as dangerous as ignoring our feelings. We need working environments where we listen to one another, consider one another, and work with, not against, one another.

Overcoming Your Inner Critic

We all have an inner critic, but some of us have louder ones. We take on belief systems from the people we were around when growing up. If we were treated as if we were worthless, or only good if we were like them, that way of thinking will have become familiar. Insufficient approval can lead to a belief that we are somehow not enough. This can manifest in a desire to prove ourselves, a longing to show those who never believed in us that we can achieve things. Yet even when we achieve whatever it is we set out to prove, it never seems enough. For many of us this is the basis for our self-criticism—our inner critic, who is never satisfied.

This letter is an example of a woman who has a particularly loud inner critic.

> I am a nearly forty-year-old woman and I've recently realized that I have no idea what would make me happy.

I'm married with children and a good career. We're financially comfortable. I have nothing to complain about. Yet the one thing I've always wanted in life is to be a writer. I've had three books brought out by a large publisher, but they were unsuccessful. So, although people say I should be proud, I see myself as a failure. I keep telling myself not to give up, but increasingly it's hard to find a reason to keep trying. I just cling to my old dream out of habit, and because it's a vanishing spark of hope in an otherwise gray landscape.

How do I learn to take pleasure in what I have, and stop feeling so empty?

This woman wanted to be a writer and is now a writer, but she has an internal voice telling her that she is a writing failure. Often, that voice is not as helpful as it thinks it is. If you relate to her and similarly have a voice that is telling you that you are not good enough, or smart enough, or whatever enough, to go after what you want—I'd like you to ask yourself, where is it from, this voice of yours? Who does it remind you of? A parent who was too scared of failure that they never attempted anything? An overly critical teacher? Somebody or something who told you external success is everything, and doing something because it works for you is nothing? Whoever it is, they may have been trying to help, but they are doing the opposite of helping. Make sure you don't stress yourself out thinking you must shine brighter, and then even brighter than that, to prove them wrong.

Our task is to recognize this inner critic. We can learn to watch it rather than assume it's right. It is not right; it is familiar. There is a difference. We won't be able to silence it, it will keep on speaking up, but we can observe it, separate it, and show it to a small soundproof cell—and shut it in. It will find a key to get out now and again, but we can just say to it, "Oh, hello, you're back. Not today, thank you." Don't have a dialogue with it or engage with it. Notice when you describe yourself negatively and distance yourself from such self-critical thoughts. They are not true, they are a habit, and they will bring you down.

Of course, we can get things wrong, but mistakes are what we must make if we are ever going to learn anything. If we make a mistake, it is a specific thing that can usually be corrected. The critical voice, on the other hand, makes criticisms that are blunt and general. It doesn't say useful stuff like, "You put too much copper oxide into that glaze so it came out black instead of green." It says instead, "You're useless, you'll never be any good at pottery." That's how you know it's your inner critic talking, and that you need to distance yourself from it.

Instead of listening to, or worse obeying, your inner critic, direct your energy into things that bring you joy. Do what you do in life in relation to your own wishes, hopes, and dreams. Sometimes we make the mistake of believing we must be good at something to do it. Luckily that was not the attitude of the community choir I joined. I didn't make great improvements in my singing, but I loved being part of a joint effort and I made some good friends. Judging yourself as either good or bad is really not the point. If you think something has to be completely brilliant or otherwise it is absolutely no good, you are also probably not looking at it realistically. The point is to do what you have always wanted to do. It can be so freeing to recognize this.

Another way that our inner critic shows up is in feelings of guilt. There are two types of guilt: useful guilt and neurotic guilt. Guilt is like a warning light on a dashboard; it is a feeling that isn't to be ignored. We can be pretty sure it is useful guilt if we can tie it to a specific behavior we are doing or not doing and it's a signal that something needs to change. But if you are doing your best and still manage to feel guilty, then it's possible that the guilt is there not because you are not doing your best, but because your inner critic has laid a guilt trip on you. This may be experienced more like angst that cannot be pinned on anything specific.

If you see yourself as a failure despite it all, and cannot silence the inner critic on that, then change your attitude to failure. It is OK to fail. It is necessary to fail. The person that never failed never made anything. Our success or otherwise has as much to do with how we talk to ourselves as it does with external factors. I think about this with regard to a man who wrote to me about his feelings of jealousy.

> I have recently come to the realization that I am a deeply jealous person, which is causing me great unhappiness.

I am envious of all my friends, my girlfriend, the stream of people I see through my social media, and of anyone I deem to even have a modicum of "success" or talent. Any positive attribute I see in someone else becomes an attribute I don't possess and therefore a negative mark on my scorecard.

My days are spent comparing myself and my work to anyone else I come across, to work out if I am more "successful" or having a better time. I can't go down the street without seeing people who are far more talented than I am, artworks that I will never be able to create, or skills that I will never be able to master.

I spend my whole time obsessing over how my own work is not as good as anyone else's. I work as a freelance in a creative industry. And everyone's work is out there for comparison. This has led to spiraling low moods and depression. How do I kill the green-eyed monster?

We cannot kill the green-eyed monster, but we can reframe it. Separate envy from jealousy. Think of jealousy as being more like when we don't want to share our mom with a sibling, or wish evil upon those we see as our rivals. And envy as being like when someone has something we want. Instead

> ### Everyday Wisdom
>
> Think of envy as information, alerting us to what we want. Envy can be a catalyst that helps us identify and motivate ambition.

of thinking of this as a bad thing, think of it as information. It can be hard to work out what we do want in life and envy is a feeling that can help us identify what our aspirations might be. Think of it, not as a pathological condition, but a normal part of mental processing that helps us realize what we want and motivates us to go after it.

However, envy can amplify our inner critic's voice. Perhaps growing up, we got into the habit of thinking of ourselves as either inferior or superior to a sibling. If so, we might now be transposing this on to all our relationships and constantly comparing ourselves. When we see someone else's success personally as though it reflects on us and isn't just to do with them, we compare their external successes to our own internal feelings of inadequacy. In other words, we are comparing people's external appearance to our inner world. My advice is to learn more about others' inner worlds. Talk about envy with friends, partners, colleagues. Learn how they experience it too. The more we keep these envious feelings to ourselves, the more power our inner critic will have over us.

Other people will always be more talented than us: Learn from and work with them rather than seeing them as rivals or potential sources of pain. If someone has a quality you feel is not even in your nature to acquire, why not join forces with such a person? It's why we work in teams—we all have different qualities to bring to the solving of problems. We don't have to do everything on our own.

If you listen to your internal monologue, is it stuck in a familiar pattern? Ask how you talk to yourself in the face of rejection. Do you think:

- Those people lacked vision. I'll change nothing and keep going.
- They were right, I'll give up.
- That feedback was hard to take on board. However, some of it was useful and I will make some changes and keep trying.

Whether we are mostly a, b, or c is likely to have more to do with all our past cumulative experiences than selecting the most productive way forward in the present. If you find yourself playing the comparison game, congratulate yourself on catching it and switch your focus. You won't improve overnight, but with practice, you can shift this over time. It's only a formed habit, and you can form new habits.

Scapegoating

Our inner critic can also get in the way of us addressing our problems directly, and instead scapegoat one problem into another part of our life. A woman in her seventies wrote to me saying that she felt consumed by regret and disappointment. She explained that while outwardly she might seem happy, calm, and outgoing, with plenty of friends and interests, this facade hid her inner feelings of dissatisfaction. She regrets marrying too young and feels she has never truly loved her husband. Sometimes she wishes he would disappear, and this feeling makes her ashamed, which is then compounded by his unfailing support of her and the steadfastness of his love even after she had an affair early in their marriage.

Following this affair, she returned to him after a few months apart because she felt lonely, and they have now been together for over fifty years. They have children and grandchildren, and she knows she has a lot to be thankful for, yet she still regrets not having chosen a life partner she feels more attracted and better suited to. She feels similarly about her career, which engages her and looks successful on the outside, but doesn't satisfy her. She wrote to me because she wanted to banish these invasive thoughts of dissatisfaction and regret and find contentment.

Thinking there is always a perfect choice to be made is a belief system, and one that can be challenged. I have a sneaking suspicion that it isn't that this woman made a bad choice in her husband, but rather that whatever choices she makes, she assumes they are the wrong ones. That's why she feels the same about her career, despite continuing to be engaged by it. Of course, we all think about "sliding doors" moments and it is normal to have some regrets in life, but I think a part of her knows that this dissatisfaction is an internal problem. After all, she did not ask for my help in finding another husband or another career. She rightly identified her problem as invasive thoughts, so she knows deep down it isn't her choices that are wrong but rather the thoughts around them that are spoiling things.

This woman's default feeling is one of dissatisfaction and her way of feeding this dissatisfaction and keeping it alive is by playing the regret game. She regrets her marriage and her career. And I wouldn't be surprised if she regretted what she chose for her AP exams or was sorry about which house they decided to live in. So what is happening here?

Our woman is playing the regret game, and there are many other games, or default ways of thinking, we can plague ourselves with. Some of us are partial to the worry game: As soon as one worry has been cleared up, another one comes into view. By playing these games, we avoid having to challenge ourselves because we believe that the cause

Everyday Wisdom

It is so much easier to blame something outside ourselves for our discontent than it is to look inwardly for a cause.

of our habitual mood is external and not internal. I'm not saying external situations and events shouldn't and won't have an impact upon how we feel. But what I'm talking about here is our default, background, habitual state or mood, and how we can keep ourselves stuck in it even if it is not a pleasant state to be in. The good news is that it is within our power to change it.

In the 1960s, one of the few ways people had of controlling severe epilepsy was by cutting the neural pathways between the left and right hemispheres of the brain. To further test this, neuroscientist Roger Sperry and his team did some experiments to see what would happen when the right and left brain couldn't communicate with each other. And what they found was that humans always come up with a reason for why they feel what they feel, and it is very often pure baloney. We weave stories and reasons around our feelings that are completely made up.

When the scientists flashed the command "WALK" into the visual field of the subjects' right brain only (by covering the right eye—the left eye connects to the right hemisphere, and vice versa), the subject got up and walked. When asked why, they invariably came up with a reason. They didn't say "I don't know" or "I felt the urge to do so" or "Your experimenters showed me a sign." No, what we do in that situation is come up with a narrative: It seems we can't help it. The subjects would say things like "I needed to get a Coke" or "I felt a bit stiff and needed to walk around." In other words, the sense-making part of the brain, which in the experiment was cut off from the feeling part of the brain, came up with a story.

We come up with reasons for our feelings and behaviors even when the hemispheres of our brains haven't been severed. And when the brain falls short of a reason, it is not uncommon to notice the nearest object or person and think that they are the reason we are unhappy.

Looking at our case study, the supposed reason for our heroine's dissatisfaction is that she married the wrong man or married him too young. Even though she felt worse without her husband than with him, she still clings to this narrative of him being wrong for her as her reason for discontent. This is because it is hard to examine our true feelings, to relive our earliest memories, and to separate our reasons from our experience. It is hard to feel our emotions without the thoughts and reasons we justify them with.

In my experience as a psychotherapist, the more emotional charge we give to our narrative, the less likely it will prove to be the true cause. If you think about it, we are emotionally neutral about facts. If I say the grass is green, even if you think it is blue, I'm not going to get incensed about your differing opinion. If, on the other hand, you challenge an opinion of mine that I like to believe is a fact but is only an idea, I will become energized and my emotions will be heightened when I reply. For example, were you to say that dogs always make better pets than cats, we will have a spirited fight on our hands. I believe that when this lady thinks about her husband, she has a charged emotion to support her habitual thought process that her unhappiness is because she made the wrong choice. She might not have done. He might be a satisfactory husband, and I might be able to come to rely on a dog for company. We get into habits with our thoughts and thinking, but they are a habit. They are not the truth.

Sometimes, instead of blaming other people or objects for other problems, we take our negative feelings and experiences out on ourselves and our bodies. Body dysmorphia is a mental health condition in which we can't stop thinking about a perceived defect about our body. It doesn't make any difference if others think it is a flaw or not—we still feel ashamed and anxious about it, and it adversely affects our life. Body dysmorphia can be the result of being teased, bullied, overly criticized, or abused when we were a child. Talking openly about our body isn't always an easy thing to do, but if we struggle to feel at home in our physical form, it is an important first step.

As an example, I received this letter from a middle-aged man who sounds like he could be suffering from body dysmorphia.

> I have a small penis. When I was fourteen or so I was called out by a boy in the school changing rooms for "having a little one." I felt humiliated. It had never occurred to me up to that point that it mattered.
>
> It seems to be something that, according to the media, is risible and makes me less of a man. The word "manhood" is used as a euphemism that equates desirable masculine traits with a big willy.
>
> I am fifty-five, a father of three, and in a happy and loving relationship with a great sex life. No doubt you would say to me that if my partner is satisfied, then I should get over my insecurity. I have much to be grateful for. I am not likely to be "playing the field" anymore.

But I worry, fret, and get depressed about this and have done so for forty years.

My upbringing was one in which I was expected to "fail" and I did develop a deep-rooted low self-worth and a sense of shame of not being enough as a person. So "evidence" such as this for "coming up short" reinforces my feelings of inadequacy. I had counseling but didn't feel I was taken seriously. I am still so heartbroken I can't "measure up" in the way that I would ideally like to. I carry a sense of real anger that it seems broadly OK to deride the half of all men with smaller-than-average penises. "Oh, he has a big car with a long bonnet—what is he trying to make up for [titter]?" How do I learn to love myself regardless of this one physical attribute that seems to me to be so crucial (and is stigmatized by most people) and forces me to hide my shame?

From his letter, it seems that his upbringing was one in which he was expected to fail and regularly led to believe he was inadequate. I don't think it is his penis size that gives evidence to this so much as that it has come to symbolize in his mind how he had always been treated when growing up. His penis has become the scapegoat for all other problems in his life. His brain made the connection, when he was humiliated about how a part of him looked in the changing rooms at fourteen, to all the times he was made to feel inadequate. The daily painful insults he has suffered up until then have all been heaped onto this innocent body part. Then every time he hears anything about small penises, in public or in private, it compounds the injury.

There are many ways body dysmorphia manifests: on specific body parts, like this man's penis, or our weight, height, sex, facial features, skin conditions—the list is endless. The specifics aren't as important as the fact that they become a symbol of our psychological pain. For someone suffering from body dysmorphia, it gets to the point where they fret and obsess about that aspect of their body, probably all the time, sometimes in the background of their mind, but often in the foreground.

Many might think, if only there was a safe plastic surgical procedure to "fix" that part they don't like, they would be cured. But it wouldn't be that simple because they would never be satisfied with the outcome: With body dysmorphia it isn't the body part that is wrong, it is the body part that is taking the blame for the psychological injuries they suffered growing up. It may feel as though that body part is at fault, or society is at fault, but really it was how they were made to feel about their whole self when they were growing up that is the fault.

Although it seems impossible to shut down that critical voice, we can develop a different relationship to it. Whether you find yourself blaming other people, or your choices, or your body for your negative feelings, to gain control of invasive thoughts, start by observing them. Accept that you can't stop them completely, but stop taking them seriously. Don't be at the mercy of your thoughts:

Observe them rather than become them and it will be easier to be unaffected by them. It takes daily practice. Make time for it. That critical voice of yours has been sending you negative messages about yourself for years, but that critical voice is not about truth, it is simply familiar.

When you become practiced in observing, you will have more clarity about how you experience your feelings and can separate them from the reasons you have been weaving around them. We don't always have a reason for feeling the way we feel. If you cannot bear the vacuum this creates (and not many of us can, we are meaning-making creatures after all), come up with a better story. The great thing about the stories we tell ourselves is that we can

> **Everyday Wisdom**
>
> We don't have to take invasive thoughts seriously: We can just watch them and not be them, and this is often the clue to a more contented life.

take charge of them. Make it an optimistic story. It won't make it true but, as I said in Chapter 1, if you are going to have a fantasy, make it a good one. If we can focus more on the positives and less on the negatives, we can steer our own thoughts.

Extreme body dysmorphia doesn't usually get better on its own. If left untreated, it may get worse over time. The standard treatments for it are cognitive behavioral therapy and/or antidepressant medication. If you relate to this description of body dysmorphia, I recommend enquiring about these through your GP. Personally, although not the standard treatment, I would favor hypnotherapy for body dysmorphia because you will need to break the connection that you have made between your psychological hurt and your body.

How to Process Trauma

The effects of trauma in childhood are far better understood now than they used to be. I unfortunately hear many stories about trauma and the impact it can have, and they all touch my heart. One man wrote me a deeply felt letter about his difficult childhood and how it continues to haunt him.

> I can't be bothered to exist anymore. I have a solid job, although it's taken me a long time and a huge amount of effort to prove my worth. I also have an amazing wife, a wonderful child, and another one on the way. But I am just existing. The only instance of spontaneity this year has been the whole family contracting COVID-19. Yes, I realize life is hard, suck it up, buttercup.
>
> I've felt like this ever since I was a child. I experienced something you must have heard hundreds of times: dad gone; stepdad abuses whole family; mom becomes zombie; my sister and I feel isolated. I obsess about either disappearing completely (barren landscape, cold,

I chop wood, no phone) or something terribly violent (being hit by a car, etc.). Another fantasy I've had since childhood is suicide, but with financial dependants it's taken a back seat.

I wish I didn't exist, that I hadn't ever existed. My whole life feels tainted and wrong. I'm certain I won't take my own life now that I have children, so I'm stuck. My wife suggests therapy. I feel therapy can only go so far. I doubt therapy could make my life less monotonous and more rewarding. Will it perhaps give me skills to embrace monotony? And accept that I should just carry on existing with the comfort that one day I won't?

I realize this all sounds selfish—children first!—but if I feel absolutely nothing, how can I put them first, no matter how much I may want to? It feels like I'm just killing time.

In assuming I had heard experiences like his before, this man diminished his trauma because it is something that happens to many people. An event doesn't need to be rare, or sensational, for it to be traumatic. When we have been traumatized, it is as though the rational part of the brain cannot talk the emotional side out of its reality. We can't "should" ourselves into feeling differently from how we do, and it's not selfish to be impacted by something so harmful. We wouldn't tell someone with a broken leg they need to suck it up any more than we should with someone suffering from the aftereffects of trauma.

In describing his mother becoming "zombie"like, it sounds to me as if she might have been dissociative and I wonder if he might be too. When life is frightening and difficult to cope with, what the body can do is dissociate. It is as though our mind and body disconnect so that we don't inhabit our own life. The emotional part of our brain gets blocked off as it continually works to keep traumatic sensations and memories from the surface. The rational part of us can go to work, earn money, build good connections and relationships, but we have nothing left to feel or appreciate that. Cutting off from feelings is a way of surviving abandonment and abuse: It is a bodily reflex. It allows our mind to leave when our body is trapped. The trouble with dissociation or repression is that we cannot desensitize to just one type of feeling without shutting off all feelings, and unfortunately it often continues long after the threat has gone. Until we know what dissociation is, and how to recognize when it is happening, it is hard or impossible to control.

There are different ways the body dissociates and there are different types of treatment available. A course of therapy that is sometimes recommended is EMDR, which stands for eye movement desensitization and reprocessing. What this can do is reconnect the emotional and rational parts of our brain, helping us to process memories and sensations, so that we can control them rather than those sensations mastering us. When we repress an experience and don't put that experience into words (or pictures), when something reminds us of that time later on, we feel the same feelings we had then. Or we feel in danger of reexperiencing those feelings and may have a flashback as though the trauma is happening now, in the present. If our feelings were of sadness, shame, or fear, it is easier for some of us to move to anger rather than dare to be vulnerable again.

It is important to put trauma into the past, otherwise the event can be lived as though it is still happening. For example, if you were injured in a bomb blast during a war because you went outside, then subsequently repressed the experience in your mind, you may continue to be too scared to leave your house even though the war is over and the streets are safer. You may even forget why you are scared to go outside but nonetheless stop yourself. It is likely that you may become obsessional about other reasons why it is unsafe to venture out. If you process the experience in a way that puts distance between then and now, you can lead a fuller life in the present and be free of your past.

When we are brave enough to keep putting the difficult stuff into words, we gradually take control over it. The more we take out the demons from their box and look at them, the less frightening they become—in the same way that the more we use a pencil, the blunter it gets. That said, there is a fine line between processing a traumatic experience to make it manageable, and reliving it and retraumatizing yourself. The psychologist Walter Mischel discovered that talking about our trauma doesn't necessarily diminish the ill effects, as is often advised, but can in fact make them worse if it is done in a harmful way.

When someone is recalling something horrific, I encourage them to keep eye contact with me so that they don't go back into the nightmare. It helps them to realize that this time they have control over the situation. Once the trauma can be put into words, it can go into the past instead of being relived as though it is still happening. Facilitating this process is an art rather than an exact science, and there is no guarantee it will work every time. Mischel devised a good technique for this. He said the effect of the trauma is diminished if subjects take a fly-on-the-wall view and write an account of the bad experience, referring to themselves in the third person. This distances them from the painful event, enabling them to be more thoughtful about what happened without being self-destructive.

There is a type of talking about a traumatic event, usually a breakup or a situation where the subject feels they have been wronged and are certain they were in the right, that sounds obsessional to the listener. When someone is obsessed with talking about their injury, it can seem like they are feeding rather than diminishing it. When we get fed up with our friends doing this, we may say that they are "milking it." This is the psychological equivalent of scratching a mosquito bite. If you don't stop scratching it, it is going to continue to itch and may become infected. The cure for this is to develop self-awareness so that we can steer thoughts rather than being at their mercy, and we can move on rather than staying stuck. It's not the talking through a problem that is bad. In the majority of cases, it is a good, if not essential, thing to do. But what isn't useful is if we keep reliving the trauma without learning to distance ourselves from it and without gaining mastery over the memory.

I agree with Mischel that dwelling on trauma may do more harm than good. But burying your head in the sand isn't going to help you get over it either. It's complicated. I highly recommend *The Body Keeps the Score* by Bessel van der Kolk to anyone interested in learning more about trauma. It explains how trauma affects the body, traces the history of trauma therapy, and describes the treatments often used, including drug, talking, and body therapies. It's a very readable book with personal stories and case studies. If we have been traumatized and still live with the aftereffect of that, it is useful to learn about all the different treatments, their advantages and disadvantages, which can put us more in control of which option we pursue.

If, like the man in the aforementioned letter, you feel nothing and can't see the point of going on, I want you to know that you will not be like this forever. Just because help you've received in the past hasn't worked, that doesn't mean you're a lost cause—it means you received the wrong sort of help. Feelings, however despairing and dark, do pass, sometimes without you doing anything.

I recently had an email exchange with a man who was on the verge of suicide because his wife planned to leave him, and he couldn't blame her for it because he'd been feeling so flat. He had scheduled an email to me that he planned to arrive after he'd ended his life. When I received it, I wrote back to him only saying to please call the Samaritans. Thankfully, he'd got the time wrong on the scheduled email and my response arrived in time. The fact that I'd written back to him altered his mood, and then he noticed a broken window latch and proceeded to spend the afternoon fixing it. By the time he responded to me, he was no longer feeling suicidal. His depression wasn't gone, but it seems that a simple email gave him just enough that he was able to find purpose and meaning for that afternoon in fixing a broken window latch, and that steered him off the path he had been on.

I wrote back again, asking him to do me a favor and make an appointment at the doctors' to tell them how he feels and about his suicide attempt. I also asked him to let me know what they said, and I'm glad to say I heard from him a little while later. He'd been to his first GP appointment, where he'd been referred to the local NHS urgent care line and the organization Healthy Minds.

This is an illustration of how a moment can pass. I'm not saying my correspondent is out of danger, but because he sent the email earlier than he planned to, and because I happened to answer it immediately (a very rare event for me), he is still alive today. And you will note, there was nothing special in what I did. I told him to call the Samaritans—which in the end he didn't even do—so the advice was not the point. A small connection like our email exchange made a difference, not what I said in it, and the main point is that moments do pass. If you find yourself in a dark, dark moment, please reach out to the Samaritans—they are there 24/7, the moment will pass.

Finding Fulfillment

We make decisions in life based on two main things: how things feel on the inside and, in contrast, how things look to ourselves and others on the outside. I call it internal and external referencing. Sometimes these two drivers can be at odds with each other. To find fulfillment, you need to internally reference how you feel more than you need to externally reference how things merely appear— even if they look worthy. I received a letter from a teacher who struggled with reconciling the two.

> Why do we define people by what they do? I'm wondering whether this is limiting my life. Whenever we meet someone, the small talk inevitably turns to "And what do you do?" For now, I am ready for that question. I am a teacher.
>
> Although there is satisfaction from the work, there is also the mental load of overseeing not only the education of pupils but increasingly their welfare, and I struggle to juggle responsibilities of family and work. I regularly think about packing it in for something that

does not take up so much headspace. Being a teacher is how I have defined myself for twenty years. How could I square it with myself if I had to describe myself with a nonprofessional job? I can't imagine saying "I stock shelves" or "I work in doggy day care." When I try to discuss it with my dad, he says he would be "disappointed because I like telling people you are a teacher."

I know I have asked my own children about what they would like to do when they are grown up and maybe I've unintentionally shown more approval when they lean toward something professional, but I now realize that all I want is for them to be happy. So, how do I find the courage to just be me, without a label? And how do I instill this in my daughters?

Many of us work hard at being seen to be doing the right thing, doing things for our résumé rather than for satisfaction in the present. If we are in the position where we can choose what sort of work we are going to do, it is important that we like how we feel when we involve ourselves in the work. That, I think, is more significant than merely liking the idea of the work. It should be satisfying not merely because it looks good to you and others, but because it feels good too.

I would advise anyone who relates to this teacher's letter to learn to internally reference more, which means working out how things feel to you, and do less external referencing—which is how things look to others. I'm not saying all external referencing is bad. It can go too far the other way too: If we don't care at all about how we come across to other people and only please ourselves, we may become incapable of the necessary adaptions that we need for the cultures we find ourselves in. However, generally speaking our decisions need to be based less on how they appear and more on how they feel. This might sound like common sense, but I'm spelling it out—the more we put this stuff into words, the easier it is to handle.

The symbols of status we hang on to are not universally acknowledged. It means little to anyone outside the legal world if you are a district judge, a high court judge, or an appeal judge because most people just hear "judge." Few would think less of anyone for having one job title or contract over another, nor are you less worthy if you are between contracts. Such distinctions don't seem important to people outside those worlds.

I see it play out in relationships as well as careers, with people remaining in unhappy situations because if things looked OK on the outside, then it would do. I remember receiving a letter from a young woman despairing that her ex-boyfriend had broken up with her, yet in the same letter she described their relationship as distant, judgmental, and their sex life as having "always been bad." However, her family would regularly comment on "how happy they seemed." Why is this enough? I don't think it should be. In general, women are told that fulfillment lies in a husband and children, and that true happiness is not found in other quarters. I think many of us have this idea, held unconsciously deep inside us, that this is what happiness is. I don't blame any woman for assimilating that dream girls are sold: that, one day, their prince will come and carry them off to a magical castle. But such an idea is only an introject (an introject is when we unconsciously adopt a cultural attitude or an attitude that comes from other people, and think that it is our own).

To climb out of this and find fulfillment, we need to unpack everything that's been implied or told to us about what happiness should look like. Then only put back what is true for us as individuals. The great thing is that this is an exciting journey of uncertainty and curiosity. We might be surprised by what we discover. I think about this with regard to a letter I received from a doctor-to-be.

> I like studying medicine because I want to help people, touch their lives, and make a change. I believe that being a doctor gives you lots of opportunities to be a useful member of society. Medicine is at the top of my list of things I find important in life because it's going to be my profession. It is a big deal as you affect people's lives in a big way. But I feel a distance coming between me and medicine, which I don't understand as I find it so important.
>
> I feel like I can easily mess up. I'm going to start my clinical rotations in the autumn and was wanting to learn some pathophysiology over the summer. I have taught myself lots of things: English, German, French, geometry, biology, and I always enjoyed the journey.

But I can't stay at my desk in order to study medicine. I feel the desire, but…well I'm just not doing it. It feels like I'll never know everything. I'll always lack information.

Everything feels too important and I can't enjoy it when it's all so serious, when it feels like a life-or-death situation. Is there a way to see medicine as less important, less serious, less risky, less heavy? Something fun/pleasant/enjoyable?

Most of us have a Willpower subpersonality and an Inner Rebel. Willpower has the words, but Inner Rebel has the action. Many times, we are familiar with what our Willpower desires, and we know what the Inner Rebel doesn't want—whatever it is that you find tedious or boring no matter how "good for you" it is—but what does it want? We need to understand our Inner Rebel better as otherwise it will only come up with excuses to avoid what it doesn't want to do.

Many experiments have been done that illustrate that old people are generally more content than younger people. We are more content because as we begin to get closer to the end of our life, we don't focus as much on the future as we do when we are young and have so much future ahead of us to think about. We live in the present and make the most out of every day because we know those days are limited. This is a lesson for all of us, to live more in the present moment rather than in what has already happened or has yet to happen. We used to have a phrase in my psychotherapy training, which is: "If you have one foot in the past and one foot in the future, you're pissing on the present."

Of course, one size doesn't fit all. If we never did any planning at all, we wouldn't be organized and go grocery shopping, and we would never have anything in the fridge to eat. It's good that we force ourselves to do homework with Willpower when we are students so that we can have a better lifestyle in the future. But I think it's important to get out of the habit of always planning and worrying about the future, and instead see that enjoying the present day can be a route to contentment. Growing older and more frail allows us to see what it is that brings us joy and fulfillment, and generally it tends to be our relationships: relationships with family and friends, with neighbors and shopkeepers, but also with old books, paintings, possessions, and ideas.

Our Inner Rebel probably wants a bit of fun, maybe some romantic intrigue, some leisure of some sort. Find out what it wants and strike a bargain with it. If we don't, our body will rebel. This probably means paying as much attention to scheduling fun as we do to scheduling our work. As Yehudi Menuhin said: "Anything that one wants to do really, and one loves doing, one must do every day. It should be as easy and as natural as flying is to a bird. And you can't imagine a bird saying well, I'm tired today, I'm not going to fly."

We are more than merely a role—a doctor, teacher, girlfriend, father, or whatever else. Don't let the idea of the role, and the meanings you make around that role, obliterate you as a person. The people around us don't just want someone playing a part—they need a real person to relate to. Be curious about whether

> **Everyday Wisdom**
>
> Learn to internally reference more and do less external referencing. Wanting to do something—liking it, enjoying it—is reason enough to invest your time in it.

your desires are internally or externally referenced. Dig into what the Willpower subpersonality part of you wants and why, and what that Inner Rebel part of you wants as well.

We don't have to choose between head and heart, we can have both. Our head can listen to our heart and take it into consideration when making, or not making, decisions. To discover what it is we do desire, I believe we must listen to both our head and our heart. There will be some finding out to do, living in the moment and asking ourselves how we feel about our experiences and allowing those feelings to be a guide, rather than what we think should make us happy.

Finding fulfillment means working out a compromise between these two parts of you. And if you find that you're stuck in a career or situation that only looks good from the outside, go back to Chapter 3 and remember it is never too late to change direction.

Our Search for Meaning

In Viktor Frankl's 1946 book *Man's Search for Meaning*, he talks about a man who came to see him who could not bear being alive since his wife died. Frankl asked him what would have happened if he had died first and she'd had to survive him. The man answered that it would have been terrible for her, she would have suffered so much. Frankl pointed out that his own suffering meant that she had been spared such pain, but at the price of surviving and mourning her. Suffering ceases to be suffering the moment it finds a meaning. Frankl could not revive the man's wife, but he did succeed in changing his attitude to his own suffering.

Frankl also quotes Nietzsche: "He who has a why to live can bear with almost any how." Existentialist philosophers argue that life is meaningless and our task is to come to terms with that. We usually try to solve the problem of meaninglessness by creating meaning out of death to soften the terror of annihilation and the bleakness of lack. A religion may offer reincarnation, or everlasting life, or fluffy clouds to sit on while playing the harp. Some of us may try our hand at denial. "I'm not scared of dying." Really? "Oh no, when I'm gone, I'm gone, and that's all there is to it." Really? "Of course, if I'm the last person alive, if my family all go first, then I'm scared of being alone, but death, oh no, I'm not scared of death." "Then why," you may ask, "do you scream when the brakes fail in your car, or when you're on a roller coaster?" We scream because we are innately terrified of death, however we try to soothe ourselves by reasoning it away or denying it really exists.

The one thing we can do is to take meaning from death. Either take from the shelf one of the ready-made meanings from philosophy or religion or make up a new one of your own. I feel that when I die, a little bit of me will live on in others because I have loved them, and I hope that they carry that love with them. This is all meaning making. I've made it out of what I feel, but I've also made it out of nothing, to soothe myself. I squirm when I say it out loud, it is but a delicate thread of a life-line, vulnerable making, trite sounding, and improbable, but, like many people who hold unprovable beliefs, I feel irrationally defensive about it.

If we look at this letter from Kate, a woman who is dying, we can see what is important to her.

> I need your help. Specifically, a woman therapist's help, in fact. Even though I've got a perfectly good and help-ful therapist, who's helped me a lot in the three years since I was diagnosed with stupid cancer at age forty-three, I'm finding that the thing I want to do is probably quite female and when I mentioned it to him, he said: "That's what women do."
>
> Long story short: happily married to a lovely man. No kids of my own, wicked stepmother to a twenty-four-year-old. I was busy-busy-busy working when I got a

terrible cancer diagnosis. Loads of chemo, loads of weeping. Grim prognosis. Still, I'm cracking on and writing this from a hotel on a jolly to London. Quite at peace with death, although obviously I'm sorry it's coming so soon. It's the living through to the end that's killing me.

I have the desire to manage my soon-to-be-former life from beyond the grave. I fantasize about music for the funeral, how to make it work for everyone, as though I was thinking about a wedding. It feels as if I am being forced to walk out of my house, leave the door open, and not mind what happens next. The cat escapes for a start, because my darling husband never closes the door.

Watching my sensitive husband watch me die is too agonizing to bear and I don't want to leave the party: We're having a great time. I think he'd quite like me to still be "around" somehow after I conk it. And I'd quite like to too. Perhaps I've answered my own question.

Should I ask a friend to send him a birthday card from a stack of forty every year? Do I leave him a box of helpful books? And sweet notes and pep talks from beyond the grave? How will any future Mrs. feel about this? She could do with a manual—he's complicated.

How can I graciously give my life away? Have you met anyone who's micromanaged their life from the afterlife? God, it's just insane.

I want to thank her for writing such a tender email showing how to graciously give our life away. It is not angry. It is beautiful. She did answer her own question and I store her lesson away for myself too. I love her idea of books, a sort of manual, notes, and birthday cards beyond the grave. I think of the results as her art, her legacy of love. In those final moments, what became clear to her is that the most important thing in her life—the thing that gave her life meaning, and gave her death meaning too— were her relationships. Her love for her husband, her love for her stepdaughter, and her love for their cat. The more I think about it, the more I realize that relationships are the most important thing in my life too. In this desire to micromanage her death, Kate is treasuring those connections and showing gratitude toward them.

What can we learn from Kate? Her death will be awful for her husband, but a beautiful funeral will make it easier to bear, and so will having familiar toilet paper. After my mother died, my father wanted to know the brand of toilet paper my mother used to buy, so that he didn't have to contend with any more change than was necessary. Such seemingly little things don't feel so little when we are grieving. "Being controlling" and planning is not always a bad thing. Kate's lists, manual, and books will not only guide her husband and stepdaughter, but they will also give them something of her to hold on to. The psychoanalyst Donald Winnicott called the teddy we leave snuggled with our child a transitional object. Something to remind them of the presence of us when we cannot be there.

Sadly, Kate didn't survive her cancer. I wrote to her widower after her death, and although he has yet to find any cards that she wrote, he has discovered another cache of things she left him—books about coping and notes about how she felt about him. These gifts from beyond the grave are his transitional objects and I am sure he cherishes and appreciates them. I imagine all this was a transitional exercise for her too, so that while she was alive, she didn't feel like she was dying all at once, and that something concrete was left of her now she is gone. We all need to do whatever we can to make living to the end more bearable and give our death meaning.

When we don't feel like we have meaning, we can be overcome by feelings of despair. I compare Kate's letter to another I received.

> I see a therapist once a week. But I have a shameful and persistent feeling of despair. I'm stuck in a miserable and futile existence. I don't like work. I hate being trapped within someone else's schedule, sending point-less emails, attending pointless meetings. I hate the nine-to-five, the long commute, asking permission to take leave—it's just sleep, work, sleep, work.
>
> I have no garden, and noisy neighbors. I won't starve or lose the roof over my head but I can neither afford to go away on vacation nor to dine out or buy clothes and books.
>
> My family and friends are wonderful. I have a part-ner who loves me. But I am just desperately unhappy. How can I say any of this out loud to the people close

to me? I feel like a petulant child: stuck, wailing. I don't know how to be alive in this world and be happy.

Some unhappiness is unavoidable. Being unhappy is one thing, but we do not have to suffer the double blow of being ashamed of our unhappiness. Many parents can't bear for their children to be unhappy, so while they don't mean for their child to find themselves unacceptable when they are sad, they may very well grow up to believe they are. If our sadness is not taken seriously when we are growing up, or if we were shamed for it, it is harder for us to learn how to be with sadness when we are adults.

I believe difficult feelings should be welcomed as they serve as a warning bell that we need to make our lives more meaningful. Meanings that made sense to us when we were younger will need to be revised as we age. It is common for some sort of crisis or feelings that are hard to bear to precipitate such a revision. Others disagree with me and would argue that difficult feelings should be tranquilized. I do believe there is a place for psychiatric drugs but not as a first port of call. It is important to listen to our feelings so we may feel motivated to enact changes that enable us to make the most of our lives.

Frankl believed that to make life worth living we each need to find our own meaning unique to us. How can we figure out what brings us meaning? I think about a letter that I received from a young man in Mexico.

I'm about to turn thirty-three. I live in a very small village in Mexico, alone in a rented house. I'm single with no kids. I work from home for a salary that just covers my bills and debts. My job is easy, but I hate it.

The last decade of my life has been all about survival. I was focused on figuring out how to leave my toxic family and violent neighborhood. My health suffered. Every day felt like hopelessness. Now I have more tranquility, space, health, and time for my own, but I still do not feel at home and I wonder if I ever will.

I have not done anything great with my life. I have never traveled, don't have a car or own a home. I couldn't afford to go to college. I do not have friends and have no love life. I read, but I am not a "serious" reader. I listen to music, but I do not know anything about it. I am not mastering any discipline. I am not getting good at anything.

I see ex-classmates who were never the smartest, but they seem content with their simple lives. Some of them own a small business, have kids, but have no aspirations. I find myself remembering when I was young, the two years I lived with my grandmother. I've never been happier than then. I felt safe and loved, and every day was an adventure. I want to feel more alive. That my life has meaning. I don't like to have reached thirty-three with nothing to show for it.

It sounds like this man has been habituated to high levels of internal stress for most of his childhood. When the source of stress stops, it can create unease, boredom, and a sense of meaninglessness. What he is going through is to be expected and it is normal. When we slow down and smell the coffee, a gap may come into view. Let's call the gap an existential void and for many it can feel a bit like panic. We don't allow ourselves to feel the slight discomfort that comes with that existential void, so we start scrolling on our phones, or turn on the TV, or open up the laptop and return to work. But instead of fearing it, I urge you to welcome it. If

> **Everyday Wisdom**
>
> An existential void feels a bit like having got off one bus, waiting for the next one, and not knowing if it will arrive or where it will be going. Don't panic; eventually a bus always shows up.

we do that, if we just sit with it, that's when an idea might come to us, something we'd like to read or make, or people we'd like to see.

It can be hugely helpful to allow yourself to feel that sort of emptiness, but instead of filling it with instant gratification (rarely gratifying in the long term), you can give yourself the chance to think new thoughts, create things, or strengthen your relationships with others. I'd like you to do some metaphorical gardening—keep that existential void weed-free, but see what crops up in it. See it as a new patch of earth where you can grow something new. And if you plant something and it doesn't go anywhere, that's OK, plant another. When finding out who we are and what we need—a lifelong task—we are allowed to experiment.

We don't have to justify our existence by flying around the world problem-solving. We are good enough to just be. Some of us find it difficult to value ourselves beyond our achievements and actions, especially if that is what we were told was important when we were growing up. We might be used to the fast lane and equate stillness and stagnation with unworthiness. Or maybe without adrenaline we struggle to feel fully alive. Adrenaline junkies often feel flat when they can't do their thing, but when they learn to notice how it feels to breathe, how it feels to touch, how it feels to taste and smell, they slowly realize they don't have to be living on the edge in order to live. Perhaps more of us would be in a similar position to this man's old school friends—content with a little business and living to pass on the love they had experienced as children—if Grandma's love was the only sort of care we ever experienced.

"Between work and sleep comes the time we call our own. What do we do with it?" asks Laurie Lee at the beginning of Humphrey Jennings's 1939 film, *Spare Time*. The variety of different activities we do is huge. We collect everything from Viennese glass to found shopping lists; we educate ourselves about things as diverse as front crawl or Chinese calligraphy. We knit, we fish, we hike, we still do amateur dramatics, and we practice and get better at it. It's good for us to get better at something and learn new things. It makes us feel more in tune with our bodies, more engaged with our minds, and more connected with our world. And I think probably the most important thing we get from these things we love doing, but do not have to do, is purpose and meaning. It's harder to get depressed when you feel you have those two things in your life.

Beginning in 1938, the Harvard longitudinal study began tracking the health of 268 Harvard undergraduates, nineteen of whom are still alive at the time of me writing, to find out what components we need in life to be healthy and content. The study has now been following the subjects for eighty-five years and was extended to include the original students' children. There are now 1,300 subjects, most in their sixties and seventies. They've gathered an abundance of data on physical and mental health, and one of the things that became clear is that people who are satisfied and content in their relationships are significantly healthier too. Embracing community helps us to live longer and find contentment. While taking care of our bodies is important, tending to our relationships is an equally vital form of self-care. We will all experience relationship failures during our lives. It is important not to judge ourselves, or to write ourselves off from them, but to learn and try again.

We are sold a dud by the media and advertising companies who try to brainwash us into thinking that success in our careers and accumulating things and money are what happiness is about. I find myself thinking, at times, *if only I had the perfect kitchen island*... even though I know it isn't a swanky modern kitchen that makes us happy or not: It's the people in the kitchen that matter. Having good and better relationships with family and friends is what we need to be focusing on. And I told that man in Mexico that what he needed to do was find and belong to a community.

Epilogue

I'm going to admit something to you: The title of this book is a trick. Yes, this is the book you want everyone you love to read because relationships are not built by just one person. It takes two people to connect and to argue. We don't adapt on our own and we have to be prepared to be affected by the people we love (and those we don't). And on the flipside, when we change and shift that has an impact on other people, and when we are more content, it's likely those who love us will be too. Our relationship with ourselves affects our relationships with others. But we cannot do anything about anyone else. While we can impact them and mutual impact is essential to growth, other people are ultimately in charge of their choices and behavior. The only person we have any real power to work on is ourselves. It's *you* I wanted to read this book.

Although we don't have control over all the circumstances of our lives—we can't choose the family we are born into, or if someone close to us dumps us or dies, or if there's an earthquake—what we always have power over is our relationship with our own self. This means that we have power over how we look after our bodies, and we have power over our internal dialogue. We have choices about how we behave toward others, and we have choices about how we react in the moment or how we reflect and respond.

In this book, I have written about the importance of relationships and the difficulties that come with that. No relationship ever did run smoothly—and I'm not simply talking about romantic relationships, because any authentic relationship will come across differences that you'll have to deal with. However difficult relationships are, though, we all need them. We need other people to be our human mirrors and to reflect back to us how they experience us, which helps us with our sense of self. Perhaps your views of the people you thought you didn't like so much when you opened this book have shifted as you've thought more about their ways of being in the world. Sometimes other people are annoying and awful, and sometimes they are simply approaching life differently than us. If we don't learn to cope with difference, either we're fighting the whole time or we collapse and lose our sense of self, consumed by what others want of us. Change is inevitable and so I hope that the chapter about it has left you more equipped when it rears its head. And although we cannot be happy all the time, if we allow ourselves to feel and contain our emotions, I hope that there will be some contentment in life for all of us.

It's a fashion at the moment for everyone to look for a box to put their feelings in—"I have so-and-so attachment style" or "my inner child wound is xyz"—and the danger of that is that they are preempting unpacking their feelings. These buzzwords and acronyms become a part of their identity and it's closing down enquiry. People aren't getting better because they are demanding instant definition before taking the time to understand themselves properly. We're all on a spectrum of understanding ourselves, other people, and our world—and to start putting ourselves into those boxes can be overdone. Sometimes a diagnosis is useful but other times it is a self-limiting exercise. You might have noticed that in this book I don't fall back on diagnosing people, and I think it's important that you avoid diagnosing yourself at the end of this too.

Becoming more self-aware and better equipped to cope with life does not mean spending every single hour of your day in introspection. It's about taking responsibility for our part in how we make ourselves feel and how we impact others. Sure, put your own oxygen mask on first. Yet just because we need to do that, it doesn't preclude us from listening to and understanding other experiences and points of view. If your introspection is leading you to more paranoia, to judgments about others, and more isolation, then it's probably harmful. If your self-reflection is leading to better connections, better communication, a calmer life, a more interesting life, and makes you feel closer to others, then I hope you will keep going. Doing work on yourself is important. It isn't selfish or self-indulgent because it helps you get rid of all the barriers that stop you becoming closer to someone else.

We are all works in progress. We are never finished and it's useful to look at different theories and see what we can apply to ourselves at any given point. Some of the theories in this book will be useful to you. Some of them will really speak to you: They will tell you things that deep down you have known all along but hadn't put into words. And some, you might not be ready for yet. Or they might never be for you, and that's fine too.

I'm not promising that finishing this book will "change your life." That is something I have wanted to be very clear from the beginning. What I hope is that some of it will prove useful to you, but it can only be useful if you get in the habit of practicing new ways of behaving and communicating. I hope it has encouraged you to look at your belief systems and responses to life and helped you decide what you want to keep—which I expect is most of your own self—and that it has given you some ideas for which new habits you might find useful to learn. Personally I'm working on acceptance and accepting my limits. I'm asking for mercy that you accept my limits as well.

When I was writing the epilogue to *The Book You Wish Your Parents Had Read*, I had a very strong message that I was desperate to get across for the benefit of human-kind. The only message I want to get across now is to be forgiving of your own mistakes, and the mistakes of others. And if I haven't covered a burning question of yours, email me and I'll do my best to answer you—either in my column or in another book.

Acknowledgments

I have many thanks to give. From Cornerstone Press, I must thank Anna Argenio and Venetia Butterfield without whom this book could not have come into being. I love these editors for their generosity and warmth, and because they always speak their minds and have faith in me when my own lack of faith would have tried the patience of saints. To my agents Karolina Sutton for getting me a great deal, and Alice Lutyens and Stephanie Thwaites for seeing it through.

Thank you to my beloved daughter who is always a generous early reader and to another early reader, Julianne Appel Opper—my dear psychotherapy colleague who kindly shared some of her ideas that made it into this book. Thanks to James Albrecht and Alex Fane for organizing my rock star book tour. To Professor Jane Shaw and the Reverend Dr. Claire McDonald, for convincing the vice chancellor of Oxford University to invite me to give the Oxford Sin of Pride lecture, parts of which are in this book. Grateful thanks go to my good friend Natalie Haynes, who suggested this book should be *The Book You Want*...rather than another *The Book You Wish*...And love and thanks to the following too: Yolanda Vazquez, Jonny Phillips, Eilidh Brooker, Richard Ansett, Janet Lee, Suzanne Moore, Lorna Gradden,

Acknowledgments

Richard Coles, Helen Bagnall, and indeed all my pals: your love and encouragement mean the world to me.

To my colleagues at *The Observer*—Harriet Green, Steve Chamberlin, and Martin Love—who edit me beautifully every week. And to all those lovely people who dare to be vulnerable enough to send me their problems, which help me enormously to think about life and how to manage it.

Finally, I must thank my dearest, darling husband, Grayson, for his love and support.

Philippa Perry, May 15, 2023

Index

Index

About the Author

Philippa Perry is an artist, a psychotherapist, a freelance writer, a TV and radio presenter, and an advice columnist for *The Guardian*. Her number one *Sunday Times* best-selling book, *The Book You Wish Your Parents Had Read*, was published in 2019 and has been translated into over forty languages. She has written two other books: *Couch Fiction* and *How to Stay Sane*. Lady Perry lives in London with her husband, Sir Grayson, and their cat, The Honourable Kevin.